Paul Burns

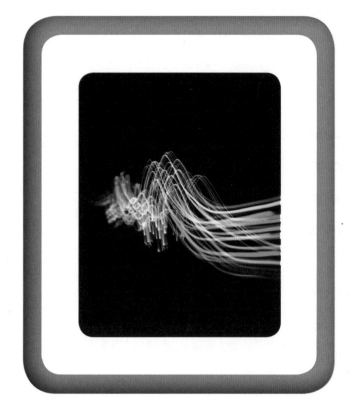

ESSENTIALS

GCSE AQA

English & English Language

Contents

Contents

The Reading Section of the Exam

The Exam Paper

Section A of the exam will assess your reading skills. In Section A you will need to:

- Read three (previously unseen) **non-fiction texts**, given to you as an **insert** in the exam paper.
- Answer **four questions** (for Higher Tier) or **five questions** (for Foundation Tier) about those texts.

Before answering the questions, make sure that you are clear which text each question is about. Most of the questions will ask you to answer on one particular text. One of the questions on the Foundation Tier paper and two on the Higher Tier paper will ask you to **compare** two of the texts.

Skills Assessed in the Exam

You will be assessed on:

- Your understanding of **form, purpose** and **audience**.
- Your ability to **extract** and **use information**.
- Your ability to use **inference** and **deduction**.
- Your understanding of how writers use **language**.
- Your understanding of **layout and presentation**.
- Your ability to make **comparisons** between the texts.

All these skills will be covered in this revision guide.

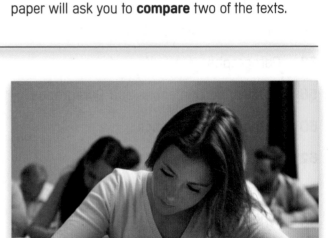

Time Management

The exam lasts a total of two hours and fifteen minutes. You're advised to spend:

- **One hour and fifteen minutes** on the Reading section.
- **One hour** on the Writing section.

You don't have to stick exactly to this, but if you take a lot longer than an hour and fifteen minutes on the reading questions, you will not be able to do justice to the writing tasks. It's very important that you attempt all the questions.

For the Reading section of the exam:

- Spend roughly **10–15 minutes reading through the questions and the texts**. It's a good idea to read the questions before reading the texts so you can highlight, underline and make notes as you read through them.

- Work out how long you should spend on each question by **looking at how many marks are given** for each answer.
  - There's a total of 40 marks for Section A, so if a question is worth four marks you should aim to spend five or six minutes on that question.
  - For an eight-mark question you should spend ten to twelve minutes.
  - For a sixteen-mark question you should spend up to 20 minutes.
- The later questions tend to be a bit more difficult so make sure you allow more time for them.
- It's always useful to have a few minutes left over at the end to **check your work**.

The Reading Section of the Exam

What the Reading Exam Looks Like

It's a good idea to look ahead now to the Practice Exam Questions for Foundation Tier and Higher Tier on pages 38–45.

As you read through this book, keep glancing at these to remind yourself of what the Reading part of the exam is likely to consist of.

Planning Your Answer

You may want to quickly **plan** an answer, especially for the questions that require longer answers.

- Don't take more than a couple of minutes to do a plan.
- Use whichever method you prefer, e.g. a **spider diagram**, **flow chart**, **thought tree** or **list**.
- Remember, a plan is purely to help you keep track of your answer; the examiner will not mark it.

Headlines — Bullet points — Columns

Colours — **Presentational Features** — Logos

Fonts — Photo-captions

Referring to the Text

It's very important to refer to the text in your answers. You can do this by paraphrasing the text or by quoting from the text.

- **Paraphrasing** means putting something into **your own words**. It's useful for summing up part of a text, for example:

> *The writer gives us a number of examples of cruelty to animals such as neglect and physical violence, which he describes in very vivid terms.*

- A **quotation** is a word or phrase taken directly **from the text**. You use the exact words used by the writer and indicate that you're quoting by putting **inverted commas** (or **quotation marks**) around the quotation. You should try to **embed** short quotations in your answer, for example:

> *The writer mentions the 'heartless neglect' of domestic animals, as well as the 'almost unbearable physical pain' inflicted on some pets.*

Using PEE

In your answers, remember to use **PEE** (Point, Evidence, Explanation):

- First make your **point** about the text.
- Then give your **evidence**, either in the form of a paraphrase or a quotation.
- Finally, **explain** or **explore** the evidence you've given.

For example:

> The writer is very concerned about what he sees as widespread cruelty to domestic animals. He mentions the 'heartless neglect' of some dogs by their owners. The use of such an emotive adjective as 'heartless' paints the owners as villains and appeals to the compassion of the readers, who would like to think they were more humane than the dogs' cruel owners.

The first sentence makes the **point**.

The second sentence gives the **evidence** in quotation marks.

The third sentence **explains / explores** the evidence.

Form, Genre, Audience and Purpose

Form and Genre

The words 'form' and 'genre' are both used to refer to types of text:

- **Form** usually refers to the **look and shape of a text** (e.g. a leaflet, book or poster).
- **Genre** refers to its **content and purpose** (e.g. a review, blog or autobiography).

Each form or genre is targeted at a particular **audience** and is written for a particular **purpose**.

Each has its own conventions in terms of **language and presentation** to target its audience effectively and achieve its purpose.

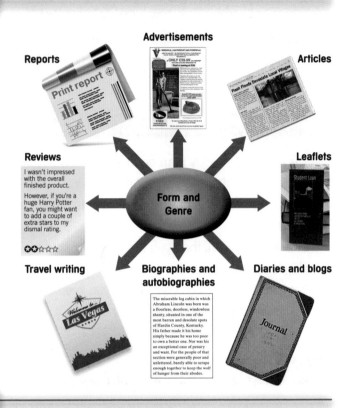

Audience

When looking at a text, you need to think about its intended target **audience** and how the writer has used **language**, **tone**, and **presentation** to appeal to the target audience.

The **content** of the text will also tell you about its target audience. For example, an advertisement for stair lifts and mobility aids would be aimed at older people, not teenagers.

Here are some examples of different audiences and some of the common features used to target them:

Children

Sentence structures and vocabulary are likely to be simplified for young children. There might also be a lot of colour and illustrations.

Teenagers and young people

Many writers adopt a less formal style when writing for this audience. Cartoons or photographs of young people might feature.

Well-educated adults

Writing often goes into greater depth, using complex sentence structures and unusual vocabulary. There might be photos but distracting presentational features will be avoided.

Specialised audiences

These could be people who do a particular job or people with a keen interest in a subject, sport or hobby. These texts often use specialised terminology without explaining them, as a certain level of knowledge would be assumed.

Men or women

Sometimes it's obvious that a text is aimed at one gender more than the other. For example, pastel colours and flowers are traditionally thought to be 'girly', whereas an action shot of a footballer might be intended to appeal to boys. These may be **stereotypes** but they are consciously used by people who produce texts, especially advertisers.

Form, Genre, Audience and Purpose

Purpose

When you are answering questions about non-fiction texts, you need to show that you understand their **purpose**. As you are reading, think about **what the writer is trying to achieve** and **what techniques the writer has used** to achieve this purpose.

Here are some examples of common purposes:

- **Inform** – the writer wants to tell you about something you didn't know. For example, a school text book informs you about the subject.
- **Explain** – an explanatory text goes a little further and looks at 'how' and 'why'. For example, a car maintenance manual will explain how to look after your car.
- **Instruct** – the writer wants to tell you how to do something. For example, a cake recipe instructs you on how to bake a cake.

- **Advise** – a text which advises looks at answers to problems and possible courses of action. For example, a careers booklet advises its readers.
- **Argue** – a text might give one opinion or more than one opinion on an issue. For example, some newspaper and magazine articles put forward arguments.
- **Persuade** – a persuasive text is designed to get you to do something or think a certain way. For example, adverts try to persuade you to buy things.
- **Describe** – many non-fiction texts describe people, places or experiences. For example, travel writing and biographical writing are often very descriptive.
- **Entertain** – many texts want to amuse or delight their readers as well as make them think.

Understanding a Text's Purpose

You can tell what the text's purpose is from:

- Its **content**.
- The **language** used – whether the language is formal or informal and the sort of vocabulary used.
- Its **tone** – for example, is it light-hearted, angry, sarcastic or sad?
- Its **presentational style** – the use of colour, images, illustrations, fonts and bullet points.

Remember that many texts have more than one purpose. For example, a biography of a well-known actress will probably set out to **entertain** its readers, while **informing** them about the actress, **describing** her character and **explaining** how she became the person she is now.

Quick Test

1. What is the likely purpose of a leaflet about an animal charity?
2. What is the intended audience of a poster advertising auditions for a new girl group?
3. What is the likely purpose of a recipe book?
4. What is the intended audience of a magazine article called *Why Does My Baby Cry All the Time? Help from Our Experts*.

Extracting Information

The first thing the examiners want to see is that you have **understood what you have read**. So, some of the questions will ask you to find information in the texts and give it either as a **list of points** or a **summary of points**. You might be asked to give factual information or to summarise the writer's views and/or feelings.

Don't assume that because a text is not fictional it must be factual. Non-fiction texts do usually contain **facts**, but they also often include the writer's and other people's **opinions**.

Facts	Opinions
Facts are statements that **can be proven** and are known to be **true**.	Opinions are **personal views**, which other people may or may not agree with.
• Writers often use **statistics** as facts to back up their arguments, for example:	• Writers might use a phrase such as 'in my view' or 'many people think', for example:
In 2009, 63% of all pupils gained a grade C or above in English GCSE.	It is my strong belief that dogs and bicycles should be banned from all public parks.
• We might need convincing that something is a fact, in which case the writer will give a **source** or authority, which we could check, for example:	• They often use **modal verbs**, such as 'might', 'should' or 'could', for example:
According to the scientific survey of the Arctic carried out by the University of Helsingborg in 1997…	This could well be the highest peak that Morrison ever climbed.
• Writers might present information without any qualification in a very straightforward way, for example:	• The use of emotive or **subjective** language, especially **adjectives** and **adverbs**, can also show that a writer is expressing personal views, for example:
The door of the house was green, with a brass knocker.	Jemima is an exceptionally talented child.
The example above is simple statement, which the reader has no reason to doubt.	The example above is an opinion presented as if it were a fact. The writer believes it to be a fact, but what he/she considers 'exceptionally talented' someone else might not.

List Questions

If you're doing the Foundation Tier paper, the first question will ask you to pick out **four important points** from one of the texts. In your answer, you need to simply **list** the facts without any explanation or comment.

For example, if your text was an article about wildlife in the Arctic, the question might be:

> List four things you learn about animals in the Arctic.

Summarising

The first question on the Higher Tier paper and the second question on the Foundation Tier paper will probably require you to **summarise**. You may be asked to:

- Summarise the facts you've been given in a text, for example:

> What do you learn about where Robinson has been and what he was doing there?

- Summarise the writer's views or feelings, for example:

> How does the writer feel about the way people treat their pets?

- Sum up the views or feelings of people other than the writer, as described in the text:

> According to Blenkinsop, what is the reaction of the people of the town to the council's plans?

You then have to find four different facts about animals in the text, which you can either paraphrase or quote directly.

If you're asked for four facts, it is likely that there are more than four possible answers but you will not get extra marks for giving more. There are only a few marks for this question, so answer it **quickly and accurately** and move on.

It is unlikely that you would get this type of question on the Higher Tier paper.

All these questions are asking you to show that you understand the content of the text. You need to pick out the **main points** and present them **clearly** in a **shortened form**.

Helpful Hints

- Highlight or underline the main points on the text before starting to write.
- Focus on the question.
- Don't repeat yourself.
- Use short **quotations** from the text.
- Don't waste time on an introductory and concluding paragraph.
- Write in proper sentences and paragraphs, using **connectives**.
- There are likely to be at least as many points to make as there are marks available.

Quick Test

1. What is a fact?
2. What is an opinion?
3. If a writer uses words such as 'might' or 'should' is he/she telling us facts or giving an opinion?
4. Why would a writer say where he or she obtained a set of statistics?

Using Inference

What is Inference?

You may have heard teachers talking about **inference** and **deduction**. To **infer or deduce** something means to come to a conclusion or work out a meaning that isn't obvious. In other words, you're 'reading between the lines', rather than 'stating the obvious'.

When you simply repeat what's said in the text or put it into your own words, you are not using inference.

Inference is a higher reading skill than extracting information as it shows a deeper understanding of what the texts are about and how they work. To get a good grade at GCSE you must show that you can infer from the texts.

When to Use Inference

The questions in Section A that ask you to extract facts from a text or sum up its main points don't require the use of inference. All the other questions *do* require the use of inference.

A question that requires you to use inference wants you to go beyond **who**, **what**, **where** and **when**, and look at **how** and **why**.

- The question might simply ask 'why' or 'how' or ask about 'reasons', for example:

> How does Julie Brown try to persuade the reader that free schools are good for pupils and parents?

> Why does Morgan Forster think Australia is the most exciting place in the world?

> What reasons are given to convince the reader to stop smoking?

- You might be asked to **explain** something, for example:

> Explain how the website uses presentational features and how these features relate to the content.

> Explain which parts of Forster's account of his adventure you find exciting.

> Explain why Harry thinks nobody will go to school in the future.

- The word **analyse** might also appear in questions, for example:

> Analyse how the leaflet uses language to persuade readers to visit Blackpool.

> Compare texts A and B and analyse how the writers use presentational features.

How to Use Inference

If you're using inference, you're coming to **conclusions** about things that aren't openly stated in the text, for example:

- The writer's feelings.
- The writer's **attitude**.
- The writer's **intentions** or purposes.
- The writer's opinions.

You can **infer** these things by looking closely at:

- The use of **language**.
- The use of **presentational features**.
- The **content** of the text – what the writer has chosen to include and perhaps what he or she hasn't included.

An Example of Interference

Read this question:

> How does Julie Brown try to persuade the reader that free schools are good for pupils and parents?

An answer that doesn't use inference, and so wouldn't gain a high mark, might read like this:

> Julie Brown says that free schools are good because 'they give more freedom' to the pupils. She tells us that it is good for parents to control schools. She also says that they would 'belong to the community'. She thinks pupils would learn more and feel safer.

This answer sums up the main points that the writer makes but it simply repeats her arguments. It tells us **what** she says, but not **how** she persuades us.

A better answer would be:

> Julie Brown makes free schools sound attractive and exciting by using adjectives such as 'innovative' and 'adventurous', while using negative diction such as 'tired' and 'failing' to describe state schools. She gives some statistics, which she says prove British state schools are failing. She cannot provide evidence about free schools from Britain because there are none but she gives statistical evidence from Sweden, showing how successful they are. She quotes many positive views on free schools, such as 'Success rates in these schools are noticeably higher', but gives no negative views.

This answer still tells us **what** Julie Brown says but it also tells us **how** she says it:

- She uses words that sound very positive to describe the free schools.
- In contrast, she uses negative **vocabulary** when writing about state schools.
- She backs up her points with **statistics** about state schools.
- She uses **evidence** from Sweden.
- She quotes the views of others, but these all support her own view.

From thinking about all these things the reader clearly **infers** that Brown is a strong supporter of free schools.

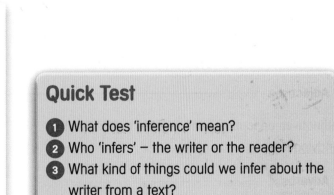

Quick Test

1. What does 'inference' mean?
2. Who 'infers' – the writer or the reader?
3. What kind of things could we infer about the writer from a text?
4. Which is the higher level reading skill – extracting information or inference?

Language

Commenting on Language

Commenting on language is one of the most important elements of answering questions in Section A.

Sometimes a question will ask you to focus on language. Understanding how writers use language helps us to infer meaning from the texts.

Diction (Vocabulary)

Diction refers to the writer's choice of words or **vocabulary**. You might notice that a writer uses certain kinds of words.

Most texts you read are in **Standard English**, written in quite a **formal style**. But sometimes you'll come across a text that uses a lot of **non-standard words**.

Slang is non-standard vocabulary, such as 'yo' or 'wicked'. Use of slang would indicate that the text is aimed at a young audience.

Dialect is language used in a particular region. You might come across words or phrases that show where someone is from.

A writer could use diction appropriate to a group of people, for example a lot of scientific or medical terms. This is known as **jargon** or **technical language**.

Parts of Speech

'Parts of speech' refer to what words do in sentences. It's important that you can identify them so that you can refer easily to them and show that you understand their function.

Nouns

Nouns are naming words.
- **Concrete nouns** name objects, e.g. chair, mountain.
- **Abstract nouns** name ideas and feelings, e.g. love, suspicion.
- **Proper nouns** name individual people, places, days of the week, months, etc. and always have a capital letter, e.g. Jane, Italy, Monday.

Adjectives

Adjectives describe **nouns**, e.g. the <u>red</u> house, his <u>undying</u> love.

Adverbs

Adverbs describe **verbs**, e.g. she walked <u>slowly</u>, he writes <u>carefully</u>.

Verbs

Verbs are doing, feeling and being words, e.g. goes, walking, lived.

You might comment on whether verbs are:
- **Past tense**, e.g. she hid, he was going.
- **Present tense**, e.g. she's hiding; he goes.
- **Future tense**, e.g. she's going to hide; he'll go.

Pronouns

Pronouns are words such as I, you, he, she, we and they.

Whether the writer uses **first person** (I, we), **second person** (you) or **third person** (he, she, they) can make a difference to how we read the text.

First person singular ('I') makes the text more personal to the writer. First person plural ('we') and second person ('you') aim to involve the reader more in the text.

Connotation

A **connotation** is an **implied meaning**. A word might carry associations which we all recognise or remind us of something. For example, red often has connotations of danger or anger, and the word 'heart' has connotations of love and sincerity.

Emotive Language

Writers choose words and phrases to arouse certain emotions in the readers. Often they use **adjectives** that have certain connotations:

> **Heartless burglars steal fifty pounds from frail pensioner Lillian Hargreaves**
>
> The adjective 'heartless' makes the burglars sound deliberately cruel; 'frail' emphasises the victim's weakness. Both words increase readers' sympathy for her.

In contrast, a writer who was not concerned about the readers' reaction might write:

> **The burglars steal fifty pounds from pensioner Lillian Hargreaves**
>
> This tells us the facts, but doesn't really affect the reader as much as if more description was provided.

Rhetorical Devices

Rhetorical, or persuasive, devices are techniques used by speakers and writers to influence their audience. They are used a lot in texts in which the purpose is to argue or persuade. Some examples are:

- **Hyperbole** (**exaggeration**) – e.g. 'Councillor Williams is without doubt the most obnoxious man ever to disgrace this council chamber.'
- **Lists of three** – used to hammer home a point – e.g. 'This building is unattractive, unnecessary and a drain on the taxpayer for generations to come.'
- **Repetition** – words or phrases are repeated to emphasise the importance of the point being made.
- **Rhetorical questions** – questions which don't need an answer. Often a rhetorical question is used simply to make the reader think.

Figurative Language

Figurative language is usually found in literary texts, such as poems. But non-fiction texts also use imagery to paint pictures in the readers' minds. For example:

- **Metaphors** – something is written about as if it were something else, e.g. 'You're a real angel'.
- **Similes** – compare something to something else directly, using 'like' or 'as', e.g. 'He was as brave as a lion but as small as a mouse'.
- **Personification** – gives human characteristics to an idea or object, e.g. 'Death waits for no man'.

Quick Test

1. What is dialect?
2. What part of speech is the word 'quickly'?
3. Why might a writer use emotive language?
4. What is hyperbole?

Presentation and Layout

Writing about Presentation

You may get a question in Section A that focuses on just presentation, for example:

> How does the writer use presentational devices to support her argument?

> Compare the presentation of Texts A and B.

You could be asked about both presentation and language in the same question, for example:

> How does the writer of Text A use language and presentational devices to persuade readers to join a gym?

An inference question might not mention language or presentation specifically, for example:

> How does the writer try to convince the reader that the rainforest is under threat?

If you get a question like this, you need to write about both language and presentation.

When you write about presentation, approach it in the same way as you approach writing about language:

- Always refer to the presentational feature using **PEE**.
- Think about how the presentation relates to the **content** of the text.
- Think about the **connotations** of images, colour, etc.
- Always focus on the **effect** of a presentational feature on the reader.

Text Organisation

You should always comment on how the text is organised.

Look for the following features:

- **Paragraphs** – if the text is arranged in paragraphs, are they long or short? Do they vary in length? Why?
- **Columns** – a newspaper or magazine article might be organised in columns, making large amounts of information easier to read.
- **Headlines** – most texts, unless they are extracts from longer texts, will have headlines. How big are the headlines in relation to the rest of the text? (Also note whether any linguistic devices such as **puns** or **alliteration** are used.)
- **Subheadings** – these are often used to divide the text into easily accessible chunks.
- **Bullet points** – these are often used to break up important information and lists.
- **Lines** and **boxes** – these may be used to make important information stand out.

Images

Some texts, such as advertisements and web pages, include a lot of **images**. Other texts may include just one or two. Look for:

- **Photographs** – think about how the photograph relates to the text. Who or what is its subject? Is there a caption? Is the subject looking directly into the camera? You can infer a lot about intended **audience** as well as **purpose** from a photograph. Photographs can also be very emotive and are often used in a powerful way by charities, for example.
- **Graphs, charts and tables** – these give information in a visual form. They can make the information easier to understand.

- **Logos** – these identify companies or institutions. They might give authority to a text as you know who is responsible for it, for example the police force or a school. Logos of well known companies can help in advertising as people are often loyal to brands they already know.
- **Diagrams** – these can help to make information, especially instructions, easier to follow.
- **Other pictures** – there could be **cartoon-style** pictures, designed to amuse you or make you think. There might be more naturalistic sketches intended to evoke an **atmosphere** or **mood**.

Other Presentational Features

- **Colour** – think about the colours used for the background of the text and the colours used for the type. Are there just one or two colours or many? Certain colours are associated with certain **moods**. For example, red can appear aggressive, while yellow and orange have **connotations** of sunshine and happiness.
- **Font** – are certain words or phrases in **bold** font or **italics** to emphasise them? Does any of the text use an unusual style of font such as Gothic? If so, what are its **connotations**?
- **Hyperlinks** – these lead to further information or perhaps to advertising.

Quick Test

1 Why might a writer use bullet points in a text?
2 Which of these texts is more likely to be organised in columns – a newspaper report or an autobiography?
3 Name two ways of emphasising individual words in a text.
4 How can graphs and charts help the reader?

Reading Articles: Reports

Newspaper Reports

Newspapers can be categorised in different ways:

- **Tabloid** or **broadsheet** – Most newspapers are now **tabloid** sized but '**broadsheet**' is still used to describe papers that concentrate on serious stories and go into more depth, e.g. *The Daily Telegraph*. Tabloids are easier to read and tend to have more stories about celebrities and scandals, e.g. *The Sun*.
- **Daily** or **weekly** – some newspapers come out every week day while others appear only on Sundays. Sunday papers tend to have extra sections, often about fashion, sport or show business.

- **Local** or **national** – local or regional papers (e.g. *The Liverpool Echo*, *The Yorkshire Post*) focus on local issues and local people.

Many newspapers are now published on their own websites as well as in print.

Newspapers contain a mixture of **reports** and **features**. The main purpose of a **report** is to **inform** the reader about something that's happened, giving some **explanation**. Opinions and arguments might be included. These will be the opinions of people involved in the story.

Language and Presentational Features

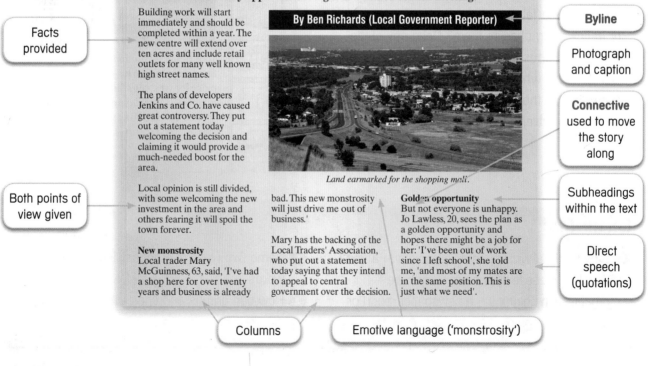

Headline in large, bold print

Strap line explaining the headline

Facts provided

Both points of view given

Alliteration of 'sh' and 'g' sounds in headline

Byline

Photograph and caption

Connective used to move the story along

Subheadings within the text

Direct speech (quotations)

Columns

Emotive language ('monstrosity')

SHORESIDE'S SHOPPING CITY GETS GO AHEAD
Plans passed at council meeting

Controversial plans for a massive new shopping mall on the outskirts of Shoreside were finally approved last night at a heated council meeting.

Building work will start immediately and should be completed within a year. The new centre will extend over ten acres and include retail outlets for many well known high street names.

The plans of developers Jenkins and Co. have caused great controversy. They put out a statement today welcoming the decision and claiming it would provide a much-needed boost for the area.

Local opinion is still divided, with some welcoming the new investment in the area and others fearing it will spoil the town forever.

New monstrosity
Local trader Mary McGuinness, 63, said, 'I've had a shop here for over twenty years and business is already bad. This new monstrosity will just drive me out of business.'

Mary has the backing of the Local Traders' Association, who put out a statement today saying that they intend to appeal to central government over the decision.

Golden opportunity
But not everyone is unhappy. Jo Lawless, 20, sees the plan as a golden opportunity and hopes there might be a job for her: 'I've been out of work since I left school', she told me, 'and most of my mates are in the same position. This is just what we need'.

By Ben Richards (Local Government Reporter)

Land earmarked for the shopping mall.

Key Words   Tabloid • Broadsheet • Report • Headline • Strap line • Byline • Connective

Questions on Newspaper Reports

A question on the report opposite might ask:

> What do you learn about the plans for the new shopping centre?

Some of the points you could make in your answer to this question would be:

- The plans were approved at last night's council meeting.
- Building will start immediately and last a year.
- It will extend over ten acres.
- The plans are controversial.

These points focus on the facts given by the reporter. The question doesn't ask about people's opinions, so you don't need to give them. A question on the same report requiring more **inference** might be:

> According to Ben Richards, how have local people reacted to the plans for the new shopping centre?

To answer this question you need to make sure that you understand all the views put forward. You also need to consider the **language** used. For example:

At the beginning of the article, Richards describes the plans as 'controversial' so we know that not everyone agrees. He describes the council meeting as 'heated', a very emotive word which tells us that councillors feel very strongly. — Use of PEE / Use of Inference

He tells us that local opinion is divided and backs this up with evidence from interviews with two people, one on either side of the argument, quoting their exact words. They both use hyperbole, the first to emphasise the horror she feels ('monstrosity') but the second to give a vision of a positive and successful future ('golden'). — Mentions language techniques (hyperbole) / Quotations given to back up the point being made

Richards also informs us of statements put out by the developers (in favour of the decision) and the Traders' Association (against). This gives us a balanced view of the situation.

Quick Test

1. Why is a 'broadsheet' newspaper so called?
2. What are the two main purposes of a newspaper report?
3. Is the article 'Shoreside's Shopping City Gets Go Ahead' from a local or a national newspaper?
4. What does a strap line do?

Reading Articles: Features

Features

A **feature article** might be inspired by something in the news, but it explores the issue in more depth. Where a report focuses on a specific recent or upcoming event, a feature may be about anything from any time.

It might **argue** a case or try to **persuade** the reader to a point of view. It could also amuse and **entertain** the reader by using **humour**.

Features appear in newspapers, magazines and on websites.

Audience and Purpose

Audience

Most features in newspapers are for a mixed, adult audience but sometimes a feature might be aimed at a particular audience. For example:

- The **'women's** pages' cover issues that are thought to appeal to women.
- The **sports** pages will be read by those with an interest in sport.
- There may be special pages for **children** or **teenagers**.
- **Financial/money** pages are for people concerned about financial matters.
- **Arts** pages are aimed at people who like music, art or theatre.

Magazines are more specialised. Many are aimed entirely at a specific readership:

- **Women's** magazines – some are aimed at older women and others at young women.
- Magazines aimed at **men**.
- **Teenage** magazines.
- Magazines aimed at **older people**.
- Titles aimed at people with particular **hobbies** from cake decorating to motor racing. Some have big readerships while others, such as football club **fanzines**, are aimed at a narrow audience.

Purpose

A feature article might be inspired by something in the news, but it explores the issue in more depth than a report.

The writer might have a strong opinion about the issue and **argue** a case or try to **persuade** the reader to a point of view, for example:

> ## TIME TO STOP DESTROYING OUR WORLD
> **Why the government needs to implement the Golding report**

On the other hand, the article could seek to present **both sides of an argument**:

> ## STILL NO CONSENSUS ON GLOBAL WARMING
> **Golding report causes controversy**

Another purpose of feature articles is to **entertain**, sometimes by using humour or a light-hearted **tone** when putting across information or an argument.

A feature article could give advice to its readers:

> **Ten Ways to Keep Your Woman Happy**

A feature article might also **instruct** the readers, for example:

> **Astonish Your Friends with this Amazing Igloo Cake**

Key Words   **Feature • Article • Tone**

Language and Presentational Features

Depending on the **purpose** and **audience** of a feature article, you might see:

- **Emotive language**.
- **Anecdotes** – short, personal stories, sometimes humorous and often used to introduce the topic.
- **Technical language** – for specialised audiences.
- **Alliteration**.
- **Humour and** irony.
- **Direct speech**.
- **Figurative language**, such as **metaphors** and **similes**.
- **Varied sentence structures**.

- **Non-standard English**, especially in articles aimed at young people.
- **Rhetorical devices**, such as rhetorical questions, **hyperbole** and **lists of three**.

As well as all the presentational devices of newspaper reports (see pages 16–17), magazine features might include:

- **Cartoons** and **graphics**.
- **Diagrams**, for example in articles about how to do something.
- A variety of **colours**.
- **Bullet points**.

Questions on Features

Feature articles from magazines and newspapers frequently appear in the exam. Often the questions include a reference to the **purpose** and/or **audience**. For example, if you were given an article with the headline:

TIME TO STOP DESTROYING OUR WORLD
Why the government needs to implement the Golding report

Then you might get a question like:

> How does the writer of this article try to persuade the reader that the government should act to stop global warming?

If the writer were on the other side of the argument and had written an article entitled:

MORE NONSENSE ABOUT MELTING ICE CAPS
Golding's report ignores evidence against global warming

Then the question might be:

> How does the writer of this article try to persuade the reader that the government should ignore the Golding report?

In both cases, you should think about whether the writer gives the other side of the argument and, if so, how does he/she deal with it – by reasoned argument or by making it seem silly?

When commenting on the language and presentational features found in an article, make sure you:

- **Think** about how each one relates to the subject of the article.
- **Quote** directly from the text.
- **Comment** on the effect of each technique.

Quick Test

1. In what sort of magazine are you likely to find non-standard English and slang?
2. Who would read an article with the headline, *Astonish Your Friends with this Amazing Cake*?
3. Who would read an article with the headline, *Ten Ways to Keep Your Woman Happy*?

Reading Advertisements

Advertisements

Advertisements come in many forms, for example, **posters** on walls, full page advertisements in **magazines**, or as **leaflets** pushed through our front doors.

Purpose and Audience

All adverts have one purpose – to **persuade**. Some may also inform. Usually the writers of adverts want us to part with money. They could be selling something or they could be asking us to give money to charity.

Sometimes adverts target people who are traditionally interested in a particular product. For example:

- Adverts for cruises are usually aimed at retired people because they often have the time and money.
- Adverts for lager are usually aimed at young men because lager is traditionally a man's drink.

Advertisements tend to have less text and more images than other texts so that they have **instant appeal** to the readers.

Language and Presentational Features

Logo to inspire confidence or affection in the reader	**Bullet points.** (You may also see other bullet symbols such as numbers or ticks.)	**List of three** highlights the product features

Other features to look out for in advertisements include:

- **Cartoons and graphics** – might be used to personify the product.
- **Symbols and characters** – many products have 'characters' associated with them, e.g. the Duracell bunny.
- Subheadings.
- **Icons** – small images, representing something.
- **Emotive language** – common in adverts for charities.
- **Alliteration**.
- **Hyperbole**.
- **Puns**.
- **Rhetorical devices**.
- **Non-standard English**.
- **Slogans**.
- Text boxes – to separate information.
- Colour – to convey mood.

Headline

Different sizes, styles and colours of **fonts**, make information stand out

Photographs of the product, and who it is aimed at

Exclamations

Direct address using the second person pronoun 'you' and **imperatives** – this makes the reader feel personally involved

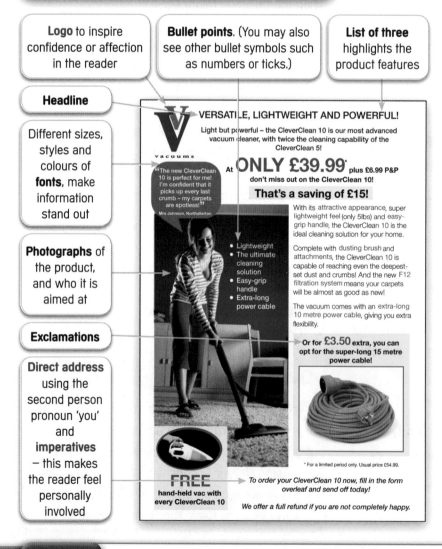

VERSATILE, LIGHTWEIGHT AND POWERFUL!

Light but powerful – the CleverClean 10 is our most advanced vacuum cleaner, with twice the cleaning capability of the CleverClean 5!

At **ONLY £39.99** plus £6.99 P&P
don't miss out on the CleverClean 10!

That's a saving of £15!

"The new CleverClean 10 is perfect for me! I'm confident that it picks up every last crumb – my carpets are spotless!"
Mrs Johnson, Northallerton

With its attractive appearance, super lightweight feel (only 5lbs) and easy-grip handle, the CleverClean 10 is the ideal cleaning solution for your home.

- Lightweight
- The ultimate cleaning solution
- Easy-grip handle
- Extra-long power cable

Complete with dusting brush and attachments, the CleverClean 10 is capable of reaching even the deepest-set dust and crumbs! And the new F12 filtration system means your carpets will be almost as good as new!

The vacuum comes with an extra-long 10 metre power cable, giving you extra flexibility.

Or for **£3.50** extra, you can opt for the super-long 15 metre power cable!

FREE hand-held vac with every CleverClean 10

To order your CleverClean 10 now, fill in the form overleaf and send off today!

We offer a full refund if you are not completely happy.

* For a limited period only. Usual price £54.99.

Questions on Advertisements

An exam question on an advertisement such as the one below will focus on **persuasive techniques**. It may ask you just to comment on presentation, for example:

> How does the advertisement use presentational techniques?

A good answer would include these points:

- The dominant colour is blue – the colour of sea and sky. Blue also has **connotations** of calm.

- The **photograph** is of an older couple; the advert is probably aimed at people of this age group.

- The man and woman in the photograph are dressed formally, look smart and look fit, healthy and happy. The readers might aspire to be like them.

- The headline **font** looks like old fashioned handwriting, perhaps making it seem personal and reinforcing the target audience.

- The smooth wavy lines could represent ocean waves.

- A bullet point list is used to highlight certain features.

- The cruise liner's **logo** is prominent. If this is a well known company, it will reassure the readers that they are in good hands.

Or you might get a more general question, for example:

> How does the advertisement try to persuade people to go on a cruise?

In this case you need to comment on both language and presentational techniques.

A good answer might include these points (as well as the points about presentation above):

- The reader is **addressed directly**, using both the **personal pronoun** 'you' ('waiting for you') and **imperatives** ('discover', 'experience').

- The **diction** emphasises luxury and comfort ('first class', 'five star', 'fine').

- **Alliteration** of the letter 'f' makes these points in the advert stand out, and also creates a soft, relaxing tone.

Quick Test

1 What is the second person pronoun?

2 What is a slogan?

3 What sort of advert is most likely to use emotive language?

Reading Leaflets

Leaflets

Leaflets can be found in all sorts of places and come from all sorts of people, groups or businesses.

They're sometimes delivered by a local group or company, or may be found inside a magazine or newspaper. They might be left on desks or on racks for people to pick up, anywhere from schools to the doctor's surgery to the local takeaway.

Purpose and Audience

Purpose

Leaflets could have a number of **purposes**:

- To **inform** people of a future event, such as a meeting or a concert, or about something as ordinary as bin collections or the local bus service.
- To **explain** things such as how to build a bookcase, or how the council has spent our money.
- To **advise** people on matters from treating illnesses to dealing with bullying.
- To **persuade** readers to buy something or do something, such as voting for a particular candidate in an election.

Leaflets which are designed to persuade their readers are **forms of advertisement** and have the same linguistic and presentational features as other advertisements (see pages 20–21).

Audience

Some leaflets, such as those which come through the letterbox advertising local takeaways, have wide **target audiences**. Others have very narrow target audiences.

The target audience affects not only how a leaflet is written and designed, but also where it's placed. For example:

- Leaflets found in schools are aimed at pupils and are about issues that affect them, e.g. peer pressure. They're written in a style to appeal to young people.
- Leaflets found in doctors' surgeries or pharmacies are usually about health matters, and are aimed at small groups of people concerned with these issues, e.g. leaflets about teething will only appeal to parents of babies.

Layout

Leaflets come in a variety of shapes and sizes. Although the whole leaflet is unlikely to be reproduced in your exam, you should try to comment on its overall design.

Most leaflets consist of a single sheet of paper perhaps with **colourful images** and a **headline** on one side and detailed text on the other. Some leaflets are folded into two or three. These might have an eye-catching image and a headline on the outside. When you open them up you might find more images and a lot more text.

Always think about the impact of the layout on the reader.

Language and Presentational Features

Leaflets are designed to **attract people** and to be read in a short time, so they share many of the presentational features of adverts, newspapers and magazines.

Look out for the presentational features listed on pages 16–21. But remember to relate the features to the main purpose of the leaflet.

The language used in leaflets depends on their **purpose** and **audience**.

Examples

Example	Presentational Features	Language Features
A leaflet explaining how to install and look after your dishwasher.	Would include **diagrams** to make the instructions clearer, as well as **headings**, **subheadings** and **bullet points**.	Would probably have a straightforward style, using **imperatives** to address the reader, and perhaps some **technical vocabulary**, e.g: Clean the outer surfaces regularly, using a soft cloth moistened with warm soapy water. The spray arms can be removed for periodic cleaning of the nozzles.
An appeal for a charity.	Might use a **monochrome** (black and white) **photograph** to reflect the seriousness of its subject matter. Inside, there could be more **emotive pictures** and **text boxes** with information about how to give money or get involved.	Would use **direct address**, **emotive language** and techniques like hyperbole, **alliteration**, rhetorical questions and **lists of three**, e.g: Dirty, dishevelled and degraded, these donkeys endure a living death.
A leaflet giving advice to teenagers about how to deal with spots.	Might take a **humorous** approach, perhaps with **cartoons**, **speech bubbles** and varied **fonts**.	Would use a much more **informal** style, still using **imperatives** and **personal pronouns**, but trying to connect with its audience, for example by using short sharp sentences, **puns** and **slang**, e.g: Fed up of being told, 'It's just your age', and, 'There's nothing you can do about it'? Take it from me, they're wrong! Follow these easy steps and zap those zits!

Quick Test

❶ Looking at the examples in the table above, identify:

a) Two examples of alliteration.

b) Two verbs used in the imperative.

c) An example of the first person pronoun.

d) An example of the second person pronoun.

Reading Diaries and Blogs

Diaries: Purpose and Audience

A **diary** is a very **personal** piece of writing. Some people make occasional entries; others write every day. Some give full accounts of events; others just give brief details. Some stick to the **facts**; others write about their **feelings and ideas**.

Usually, the intended **audience** of a diary is the writer. People write diaries to remember events in their lives, or as an outlet for their feelings.

Language and Presentational Features

If you're given an extract from a diary in your exam, it's unlikely that you'll be expected to comment on presentational features.

The text is usually organised in **chronological order** under **headings** which give the **date**. There may be **footnotes** explaining references and perhaps **photographs** or other **illustrations**.

Some language features you might find in a diary extract include:

- Use of the **first person** (I, me, our) – this is the writer's own story seen from his/her own point of view.
- **Direct speech** – conversations may be quoted.

- **Informal language**/**slang** – some diarists write the way they speak.
- **Formal language** – some diarists write in **Standard English** and in carefully constructed sentences.
- **Literary language** – some use a lot of descriptive and **figurative language**.
- A range of **tenses** – diarists usually use the **past tense**, but may switch to the **present tense** to make the scene more immediate, as if it's being relived. They also use the present tense to reflect on events and express their feelings.

Example: *The Diary of Samuel Pepys*

In this extract from *The Diary of Samuel Pepys*, Pepys describes the Great Fire of London in 1666.

What might you be able to say about Pepys's use of language and how it shapes the reader's response?

- Use of the **first person** shows that he witnessed it all.
- There is **no main verb** in the first sentence.
- Pepys builds up a picture of activity with a long sentence, using a series of **present participles**.
- **Alliteration** and **assonance** are used to emphasise the scene.

Everybody endeavouring to remove their goods, and flinging into the river or bringing them into lighters that lay off; poor people staying in their houses as long as till the very fire touched them, and then running into boats, or clambering from one pair of stairs by the waterside to another. And among other things, the poor pigeons, I perceive, were loth to leave their houses, but hovered about the windows and balconies, till they some of them burned their wings and fell down.

Chronological • Direct speech • Figurative language • Past tense • Present tense • Assonance

Blogs: Purpose and Audience

A **blog** is an online diary. Entries appear in **reverse chronological order** – you read the latest entry first.

Like diaries, blogs:
- Are personal, usually the work of one person.
- Can include events, feelings and opinions.
- Are kept up-to-date.

Unlike diaries, blogs:
- Are always intended to be read by others.

- Are published immediately electronically.
- Invite responses from readers, and so can be a form of social networking.
- Can be published by companies and groups, as well as by individuals.
- Might focus on an issue or subject area.

The purpose of a blog can be to inform, entertain, describe, argue, explain, persuade or advise.

Language and Presentational Features

Some very informal blogs might use 'text language', with initials, **phonetic spellings**, symbols and emoticons.

One interesting difference from most other text types is that usually when a **blogger** asks a question, it **isn't** a rhetorical question. He/she genuinely wants a reply.

Image (often photos are used but not as many as in most websites).

Hyperlink, connecting to other websites.

Text box (often contains adverts for the writer's product or something they endorse).

GUI (graphic user interface) **widgets** invite the readers' comments.

Headlines (and **subheadings**).

Blocks of text arranged in **paragraphs**.

Written in **Standard English**.

Question

Mike's Film Blog
September

The film of the book? No thanks.

I was watching The Lord of the Rings the other day and had two nearly simultaneous thoughts:

1. This is the best adaptation of a book I have ever seen.
2. It's nowhere near as good as the book.

I know a book like The Lord of the Rings is especially difficult with all the special effects and stuff but I think both my thoughts work. Books do make good sources for films but no film has ever lived up to its source material.

The reason for this is simple; the mind's eye beats Technicolor, IMAX and 3D every time. I can imagine things at virtually no cost to myself that it would take a film maker years of effort, enormous talent and squillions of dollars to produce.

So why do we go to the cinema when we've got so much going on in our heads?

Leave a comment:

About this blog

Every month, Mike discusses issues in the world of films.

This month, which is better - books, or films of books?

Questions

If you were given the blog above in your exam, you might be asked:

> What arguments are put forward in 'Mike's Film Blog' to support the idea that films are never as good as the books on which they are based?

This question asks you to identify the main points that Mike makes and summarise them.

> How does Mike try to start a debate about the relative merits of books and films?

This question requires you to comment on Mike's use of both linguistic and presentational features.

Quick Test

1. Looking at 'Mike's Film Blog' answer these questions:
   a) What 'person' is the blog written in?
   b) What is the purpose of the green text box?

Reading Biography and Autobiography

The Difference Between Biography and Autobiography

A **biography** is the story of someone's life.
An **autobiography** is the story of someone's life written by him/herself.

Biographies:

- Can be written when the subject is still alive or after he/she is dead.
- Can be '**authorised**' (the subject has cooperated with the writer) or '**unauthorised**' (the writer has written the book without the subject's approval).
- Are usually based on research by the author — perhaps from historical records or from interviews.

Autobiographies:

- Can only be written when the subject is alive.
- Are based on memory, perhaps backed up by some research.
- Are sometimes written by someone other than the subject, who may not be acknowledged (**'ghost' writers**).

Some books are based on someone's real life experience but also include made-up characters and events so they're partly autobiographical and partly **fictional**.

Purpose and Audience

Purpose

Biographical and autobiographical writing has several purposes:

- To **inform** us about a person's life — a new biography will often tell us things we didn't already know.
- To **explain** how people grew up and developed.
- To **describe** people and places.
- To **entertain** — real life stories can be as exciting or amusing as any work of fiction.
- To **argue** and **persuade** — a biographer might present controversial ideas about a well-known person or events in history.

Audience

The **target audience** of biographies and autobiographies is anyone who is interested in the person.

Particular subjects are expected to appeal to certain readers so the style of writing might be adjusted to suit them. For example:

- A biography of Justin Bieber would mostly appeal to young girls and would probably be written in fairly simple, informal language, with lots of photos.
- A biography of Charles Dickens could also contain photographs, but it would be written in **Standard English**, with lots of footnotes and a bibliography.

It's likely that the biography of Dickens would be much more critical than that of Bieber. But, it's possible that someone could produce a critical biography of Justin Bieber in the future. Similarly, there have been simplified biographies of Dickens aimed at younger readers.

  **Key Words**   **Biography • Autobiography • Authorised • Unauthorised • Ghost writer**

Reading Biography and Autobiography

Language and Presentational Features

Language

Some language features you might find in autobiographies and biographies include:

- Autobiographies, like diaries, are written in the **first person** (I, we). Biographies are written in the **third person** (he, she, it, they).
- **Descriptive** and **figurative language** helps to create a sense of time and place.
- **Standard English** is likely to be used in the narrative but **slang** and especially **dialect** could be used occasionally to give an authentic 'feel'.
- Most biographical writing is in the **past tense**, but the **present tense** might be used to try to make the readers feel as though they're experiencing something as the subject experienced it.

- Some autobiographies employ a **colloquial** or 'chatty' style. This might make us feel that we have a friendly relationship with the subject.
- **Direct speech** and **indirect speech** may be used to create different effects.
- In more academic biographies **footnotes** tell us where the writer got the information.

Presentation

Biographies and autobiographies don't tend to include many interesting presentational features. There could be a **photograph**, which might tell us something about the subject's life. **Sketches** or **diagrams** (e.g. family trees) might also feature.

Example: *Father and Son*

This is an extract from *Father and Son*, an autobiography by Edmund Gosse, in which Gosse describes his early childhood.

> How does Gosse use language to tell us about his early childhood?

> Out of the darkness of my infancy there comes only one flash of memory. I am seated alone, in my baby-chair, at a dinner-table set for several people. Somebody brings in a leg of mutton, puts it down close to me, and goes out again. I am again alone, gazing at two low windows, wide open upon a garden. Suddenly, noiselessly, a large, long animal (obviously a greyhound) appears at one window-sill, slips into the room, seizes the leg of mutton and slips out again.

Use of the **present tense** makes the scene more real and vivid.

The **personal pronouns** 'I' and 'me' are used, which give the story a personal, **anecdotal** feel.

Adjectives and descriptive language are used to provide a clear image of the scene.

A **long sentence** is used to build up to the point of the story.

Quick Test

1. Look again at the extract from *Father and Son*.
   a) Why does Gosse describe the memory as coming 'out of the darkness'?
   b) Why do you think he writes in the present tense?
   c) Why would he say 'somebody' and not name the person?
   d) What adverb is used to describe the dog's entrance and why is it effective?

Reading Travel Writing

Travel Writing

Travel writing can be found in two forms:
- A **guide book**, giving information about a place.
- An **autobiographical** account of a journey – from a coach trip around Britain to an expedition to the South Pole.

Purpose and Audience

Purpose

A travel guide:
- **Informs** readers about transport, hotels, restaurants and tourist attractions.
- **Explains** how to get around and how to do things like ordering food in another language.
- **Advises** readers about the best options for them, and what to do in an emergency.
- **Describes** the destination.
- May **persuade** readers to go somewhere different or do something new.

Autobiographical travel writing:
- **Entertains** its readers.
- **Describes** the writer's travels and adventures.
- **Informs** the readers about the places visited.
- **Explains** different cultures and lifestyles.

Audience

The main target audience for a travel guide is people who are planning to go to a place. Some guides are aimed at people who like luxury; others are for those travelling on a budget.

Autobiographical travel writing, on the other hand, tends not to be aimed at a specific audience.

Language and Presentational Features

Presentation

A long piece of autobiographical travel writing, in the form of a book, is usually divided into **chapters**, written in **paragraphs** and accompanied by **photographs**, and perhaps by **maps** and **sketches**.

A shorter piece could appear in a magazine or newspaper, perhaps laid out in **columns**, with a **headline** and **subheadings**. It might also include a photograph or a map.

Travel guides have a lot of **illustrations**, maps and plans and less text. They use **columns**, **bullet points**, **icons** and **text boxes**. They usually include plenty of **photographs** and **colour**.

This kind of travel writing can also be found in newspapers and magazines. The writer visits a country, city or resort and reviews it, giving views on the area, hotels, restaurants and leisure activities. Such articles give personal opinions, and sometimes they're a form of advertising (in which case they're always positive.)

Language

The language of autobiographical travel writing is **personal** and **descriptive**. It may also use quite scientific or **technical language** when, for example, describing in detail the ascent up a cliff face.

Travel guides are less personal, as they usually aim to give **unbiased accounts** of the places they describe. They often address the reader directly when giving advice. At other times they might use very **descriptive language** – even **hyperbole** – when describing the scenery or architecture.

Example: Extract from a Guide Book

Here is a guide book extract for Lake Garda, Italy.

How are language and presentation used to inform, advise and persuade readers?

Use of **adjectives** make the lake sound attractive and appealing

List of three highlights the beautiful scenery

Presentation of **facts** makes the writer sound knowledgeable and trustworthy

Lake Garda is Italy's largest lake, a beautiful expanse of blue originally caused by glaciation.

The glorious surrounding scenery varies from dramatic snow-capped mountains to tranquil sandy shores and soft vine-covered hills. The stunning setting has led to Lake Garda becoming one of Italy's most popular tourist destinations, an ideal spot for sunbathing and water sports.

We recommend:

🛏

Hotel Paradiso, Densanzo	★★★★★
Hotel Internationale, Garda	★★★
Pensione La Mama, Peschiera	★

🍴

Da Gusto, Garda	£££££
Osteria Almeria, Sirmione	£££
Trattoria Rosa, Salo	££

Use of **tables** to organise information clearly

Icons are used to rate the hotels and restaurants

Example: *Pictures from Italy*

This is an extract from Charles Dickens's *Pictures from Italy*, where he describes the city of Genoa.

How does Dickens use language to re-create the atmosphere of Genoa?

First person makes it sound personal

Negative diction such as 'rottenness' and 'deformed' give vivid images

Enthusiastic **listing** of all the things that hang out of the windows helps to make the scene come alive

One of the rottenest-looking parts of the town, I think, is down by the landing-wharf: though it may be, that its being associated with rottenness on the evening of our arrival, has stamped it deeper in my mind. Here, again, the houses are very high, and are of an infinite variety of deformed shapes, and have ... something hanging out of a great many windows, and wafting its frowsy fragrance on the breeze. Sometimes, it is a curtain; sometimes, it is a carpet; sometimes, it is a bed; sometimes, a whole line-full of clothes; but there is almost always something.

Present tense makes the scene seem real

Alliteration emphasises certain words

Repetition highlights the writer's feelings

Quick Test

1. Look again at the two extracts above. Which one:
   a) Gives information that might be useful to a tourist?
   b) Is written mainly to entertain the reader?
   c) Gives us a sense of the presence of the writer?
   d) Is designed partly to advise the reader?

Reading Reviews

Reviews

A **review** gives one person's opinion about anything from a film or a concert to a hotel.

Reviews may be written just after a new product comes out (e.g. for books and games) or soon after the first showing of a film, play or TV programme. Restaurant and hotel reviews might be written at any time.

You might also come across **previews**. These are articles written **before** the product can be seen by the public.

Reviewers are also known as **critics** because they give their **critique** on what they're writing about. Critics say what they think – good or bad.

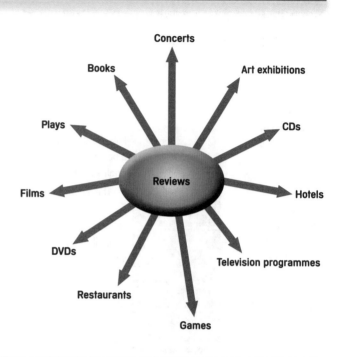

Purpose and Audience

Purpose

Reviews can have a number of purposes:
- The main purpose of a review is to **argue** the critic's point of view. The critic gives his/her opinions and backs them up with evidence.
- It also **informs** the reader about whatever is being reviewed, maybe giving details of times, dates and prices.
- If the review is positive it might **persuade** readers. Many people make decisions based on reviews. They might trust one particular critic or read several reviews.
- Reviews are also read by people who read them purely for **entertainment** because they're witty or controversial.

Audience

Target audiences vary according to where the review is published. You find reviews in:
- Newspapers, both tabloid and broadsheet.
- Magazines, including specialist magazines.
- Academic journals (for students and teachers).
- Blogs and other websites.

The target audience of the publication determines what is reviewed. A local newspaper would review local plays and local restaurants; national newspapers focus more on London. Books and films are reviewed in newspapers nationwide.

Broadsheets include a much greater range of reviews than tabloids. They contain reviews for things that might only appeal to a small audience, while tabloids concentrate on products with mass appeal.

Presentational and Language Features

When reading reviews, look out for the presentational features you'd expect to find in most newspaper and magazine articles:

Headline – makes the review stand out, sometimes indicates the critic's reaction

Byline – the reviewer's identity can make a difference to how the reader might react

Present tense

THIS 'OLIVER' WILL HAVE YOU BEGGING FOR MORE!

'Oliver!' at the Palace Theatre until March 31st.

by Joe Skinner

★★★★★

THE AUDIENCE was standing and cheering at the end of this show and the ovation was well-deserved. It is a triumph from start to finish.

This all-new production by local company *The*

Vagabonds is not to be missed. It makes the well-known story seem fresh and relevant.

Tom Brown's truly menacing Fagin slavers like a hungry wolf in his scenes with young Julian Forbes-Smith's Oliver, and the rest of the cast is almost faultless.

Strap line – gives extra information. (This sort of information is sometimes found at the bottom of the review.)

Ratings – using icons, e.g. stars

Columns

Other features to look out for in reviews include:
- **Subheadings**.
- **Photographs**/**illustrations** – film, TV and theatre reviews often include photos.
- **First person** – some reviewers put themselves into the review, e.g. 'I had the pâté'.
- **Puns** and **word play**.

- **Imperatives** – some reviews address the readers directly, e.g. 'Don't miss it!'.
- **Figurative language** – **metaphors** and **similes** are often used to put vivid images into the readers' minds.
- **Hyperbole** – exaggeration is often used to emphasise the writer's thoughts.

Questions

If you were given the review above in your exam, you might be asked:

> What are Joe Skinner's thoughts and feelings about 'Oliver'?

This question asks you to identify the writer's thoughts and feelings about the play and summarise them.

> How does Joe Skinner express his opinions about 'Oliver'?

This question asks you to explain how the writer gets his opinion across to the reader. Look for use of language techniques such as hyperbole, superlatives, sarcasm, positive or negative diction.

Quick Test

1 Read the review above and identify: **a)** A simile   **b)** Hyperbole

Reading Web Pages

The Web

The **worldwide web** means that now almost everything that, in the past, would have been printed on paper is published on the web.

Some texts appear on the web as well as in print (**hard copy**); others appear only on the web.

Advantages of the Web	Problems with the Web
For writers: • It reaches a huge, worldwide audience. • Texts can be published instantly. • Texts can be changed and updated easily. For readers: • It's cheap and easily accessible. • Texts are easy to find and often lead, via links, to other texts. • It can be **interactive**.	• There's so much material available, it can be hard to find what you want. • It isn't always clear who's responsible for a website. For example, it might look as if it's the work of an individual when, in fact, it's published by an interest group. • Information can be unreliable or out-of-date.

Purpose and Audience

Because any kind of text can be published as web pages, their audiences and purposes are very diverse. The web is a **medium**; through it we can access many genres in many forms.

Most organisations and companies and many individuals have websites. Their purposes are:

• **To inform** – websites such as Wikipedia, an internet **encyclopedia**, are amongst those often used. Schools, newspapers and news organisations (e.g. the BBC) use websites to inform.

• **To persuade** – **internet shopping** is growing and companies have websites to persuade us to buy from them. Charities also make use of the web.

• **To argue** – opinion pieces most often come in the form of blogs (see page 25). Political parties and pressure groups also use web pages.

• **To advise** – websites can give advice, e.g. medical advice. (A lot of doctors aren't keen on these sites; they can be unreliable.)

• **To entertain** – some sites are purely for entertainment; some have other primary purposes but also provide entertainment.

Language and Presentational Features

Language

The language used on web pages depends on their **purpose**, their target **audience**, and their **genre**. A web page can be an electronic version of:

• A newspaper or magazine article.
• An advertisement.
• An information leaflet or brochure.
• A dictionary or encyclopedia.
• A diary.
• An advice sheet or problem page.

The language used will be no different from the language used in the hard copy equivalent.

Key Words   **Worldwide web • Hard copy • Interactive • Encyclopedia**

Language and Presentational Features (Cont.)

Presentation

If you're given a web page in the exam, the most important thing to remember is to comment on the **whole page** – look at all the surrounding text boxes, links, etc.

Example of a Web Page

This is a page from the Dogs Trust website.

How does the web page encourage the reader to support the work of the Dogs Trust?

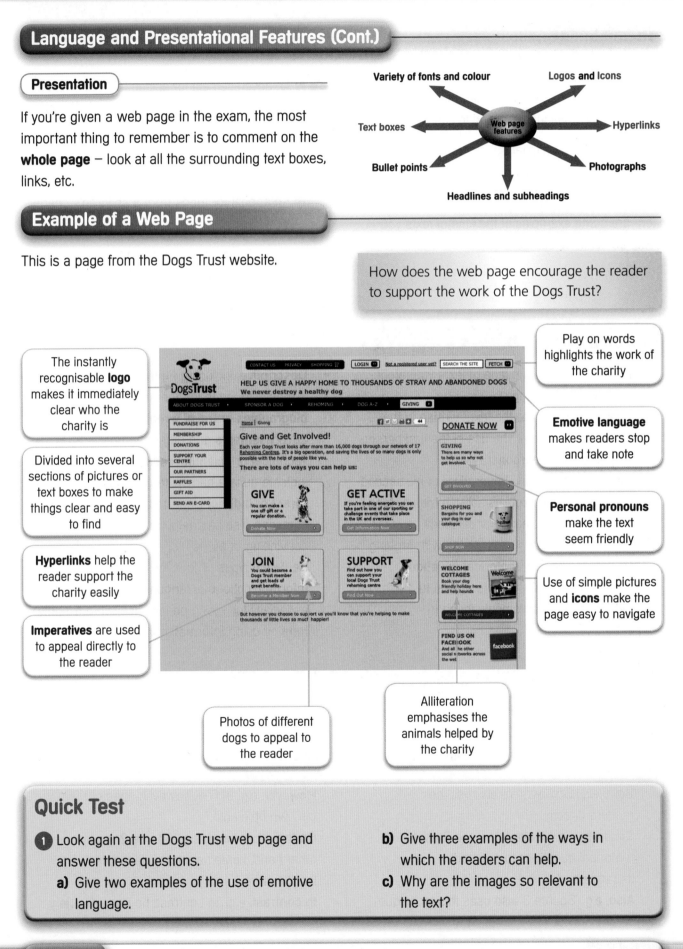

The instantly recognisable **logo** makes it immediately clear who the charity is

Divided into several sections of pictures or text boxes to make things clear and easy to find

Hyperlinks help the reader support the charity easily

Imperatives are used to appeal directly to the reader

Play on words highlights the work of the charity

Emotive language makes readers stop and take note

Personal pronouns make the text seem friendly

Use of simple pictures and **icons** make the page easy to navigate

Photos of different dogs to appeal to the reader

Alliteration emphasises the animals helped by the charity

Quick Test

1. Look again at the Dogs Trust web page and answer these questions.
   a) Give two examples of the use of emotive language.
   b) Give three examples of the ways in which the readers can help.
   c) Why are the images so relevant to the text?

Comparing Language

Comparing Language

You'll always get a question in the exam that asks you to **compare** two of the texts. Often this question focuses on how language is used to achieve purpose.

The texts will have similar subject matter but they will have been written for different **purposes** and/or with different **audiences** in mind.

Here are some examples of the kind of texts you could be asked to compare:

1 **A:** An advertisement for guided tours of China **and**
B: A newspaper article about Chinese industry.

2 **A:** An extract from the autobiography of a famous person who was brought up in a children's home **and**
B: An appeal for funds from a children's charity.

3 **A:** A magazine article for teenagers about the dangers of plastic surgery **and**
B: A light-hearted newspaper feature about celebrity plastic surgery.

What to Look For

When comparing the language of texts you might comment on the following:

- **Narrative voice** – are the texts written in the **first or third person**? The use of the first person tells you a text is **personal**.
- **Direct address** – using **imperatives** or the **second person** (you). This might establish a **friendly tone** or might be used to advise or persuade.
- **Rhetorical** language – associated with arguing and persuading, e.g. **rhetorical questions**.
- **Emotive language** – used to appeal to the readers' feelings; commonly found in persuasive texts.

- **Descriptive**, including **figurative**, language – mostly found in longer texts such as **biographies** or **travel writing**, but also used in **advertisements** and other persuasive texts.
- **Technical** or **scientific vocabulary** – might indicate quite a narrow target audience.
- **Direct** or **indirect** (reported) **speech** – quoting someone else can help make the text more convincing or authentic.
- **Sentence types** – does the text include a variety?
- **Informal/colloquial language** – some texts, especially for young people, achieve a **friendly tone** by using **informal**, **non-standard** English.

Useful Words and Phrases

This table lists some words and phrases that you may find useful when comparing texts.

Discussing Similarities	Discussing Differences
• **Both**, e.g. 'Both writers address their readers directly'. • **Similarly**, e.g. 'Similarly, source 2 uses rhetorical questions to persuade its readers…'. • **Also**, e.g. 'Source 3 also uses this technique'.	• **However**, e.g. 'Jones, however, does not give his own opinions'. • **On the other hand**, e.g. 'Source 2, on the other hand, contains a lot of descriptive language'. • **In contrast**, e.g. 'In contrast, he uses a variety…'.

Approaching the Question

When answering the question, make sure you:

- Comment on **similarities** *and* **differences**.
- Relate your comments to **purpose** and **audience**.
- Use plenty of short **quotations** from the texts.
- Use **PEE**.
- Consider the writers' **attitudes**.

If the question asks you to compare only the writers' use of language, **do not** write about presentation.

Comparing Language: An Example

Look at these two extracts from texts about travel.

Source 1

Lake Garda is Italy's largest lake, a beautiful expanse of blue originally caused by glaciation.

The glorious surrounding scenery varies from dramatic snow-capped mountains to tranquil sandy shores and soft vine-covered hills. The stunning setting has led to Lake Garda becoming one of Italy's most popular tourist destinations, an ideal spot for sunbathing and water sports.

Guide to the Italian Lakes

Source 2

One of the rottenest-looking parts of the town, I think, is down by the landing-wharf: though it may be, that its being associated with rottenness on the evening of our arrival, has stamped it deeper in my mind. Here, again, the houses are very high, and are of an infinite variety of deformed shapes, and have… something hanging out of a great many windows, and wafting its frowsy fragrance on the breeze. Sometimes, it is a curtain; sometimes, it is a carpet; sometimes, it is a bed; sometimes, a whole line-full of clothes; but there is almost always something.

Pictures from Italy, Charles Dickens

Consider the following question:

> Compare the different ways in which language is used for effect in the two texts. Give some examples and analyse what the effects are.

In answering the question you could mention that:

- Dickens uses the **first person** to state his opinions, while the guide is quite **impersonal**, which makes it seem reliable.
- Dickens makes it clear that he is giving a **personal view** ('I think') while the description in the guide is presented as being **factual**, again making it seem reliable.
- Both texts are highly **descriptive**, but the first one uses a lot more **adjectives**, ('dramatic', 'soft') designed to make the place seem attractive.
- The **diction** of the guide book is entirely positive, which will encourage readers to visit, while some of Dickens's language could give a negative impression of the town.
- Both use **alliteration** to highlight certain points.
- Dickens uses **long sentences** and **repetition**, giving an almost hypnotic effect ('sometimes…') to involve the reader.

Quick Test

1 Look at the three examples of texts given on page 34 and answer the following questions with Text A, Text B or Both.

   a) Which text in example 1 is likely to use technical vocabulary?

   b) Which text in example 2 is likely to use emotive language?

   c) Which text in example 3 is likely to address the reader directly?

Comparing Presentation

Comparing Presentation

If the comparison question in the exam doesn't focus on language, it will probably focus on presentation. Not all the texts which you are given will have many presentational features that you can comment on.

You're more likely to be asked to compare presentational features if you're taking the Foundation Tier paper than if you're taking the Higher Tier paper.

Just as you would when comparing language, firstly you should think about the **purpose** and **audience** of the two pieces. The presentational features used in each text depend on its purpose and audience.

Here are some examples of the kind of texts you could be asked to compare:

1 **A:** A leaflet giving advice about safety in the home **and**

B: A magazine article by a woman whose house fell off a cliff.

2 **A:** A leaflet advertising a local zoo **and**

B: An advertisement appealing for funds from an animal charity.

3 **A:** A page from a school website detailing the school's achievements **and**

B: A blog called *The Truth About School* written by teenagers.

What to Look For

When comparing presentational features, you might ask yourself these questions:

- How much **text** is there on each page?
- How is the text set out – in **columns** or in blocks, or perhaps in **text boxes**?
- How is the text organised – in conventional paragraphs or with **bullet points**, numbers or other devices?
- Are there **headlines**, **subheadings**, **bylines** and **strap lines**?
- What sizes and styles of **font** are used? Is the font the same throughout?
- Is there any **colour** or is the whole thing **monochrome**?

- Is colour used for the background and, if so, does it help to create a **mood**?
- Are there **photographs**? How many photographs are there and how do they relate to the text?
- Are there any **other illustrations** and how do these relate to the text?
- Are there any **logos** or **icons**?
- Are there any **graphs**, **charts** or **diagrams**?
- Is there any material on the page that isn't strictly relevant to the text? If so, why?

If you see that one, or both, of the texts uses any of these presentational devices, think about how they relate to the text and what effect they have on the reader.

Text box • Monochrome • Graph • Chart • Diagram

Approaching the Question

When answering the question, make sure you:
- Comment on both **similarities *and* differences**.
- Use **PEE**, just as when commenting on language (the 'evidence' would be a description of a presentational feature, rather than a quotation).

- Relate your comments to the texts' **purpose** and **audience**.

If the question specifically asks you to compare only the writers' use of presentational features, **do not** write about language.

Comparing Presentation: An Example

Look at these two texts, both about aspects of law and order and consider the following question:

> Look at Sources 1 and 2 and compare the presentational features. Remember to:
> - Write about the way the sources are presented.
> - Compare how they look.

Source 1

Source 2

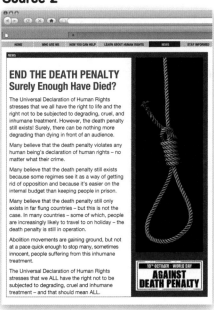

In answering the question you could mention that:
- Source 2 has a lot more text than source 1.
- Both have one **dramatic image**, but in text 1 it is central, dominating the leaflet, while in text 2 it's at the side, complementing the text.
- Source 1 has white print on a red background, indicating danger. Source 2's text is mainly black and white but the **headline** is red, which has **connotations** of blood and death.
- Source 1 uses a drawing of a large hand crushing a car, which echoes the **headline**, and emphasises the police's power.
- Both texts include **logos** to show who produced them and that they're part of a campaign.
- Source 1 is a **leaflet** while source 2 is a **web page** and includes **hyperlinks** along the top.

Quick Test

1. Look at the three examples of texts given on page 36 and answer the following questions with Text A, Text B or Both.

    a) Which text in example 1 is most likely to be set out in columns?

    b) Which text in example 2 would be more likely to use bright colours?

    c) Which text in example 3 is more likely to feature photographs of hard working pupils?

Exam Practice Questions: Foundation Tier

Section A of the Foundation Tier exam will consist of five questions: 1, 2, 3, 4 and 5. Here are examples of these questions.
- *Answer all the questions.*
- *You are advised to spend 1 hour 15 minutes on these questions.*

Read **Source 1**, the magazine article called *My House Fell Off A Cliff!* by Frances Lowe, and answer the questions below.

1. List four things you learn about Frances's house and what happened to it.   *(4 marks)*

2. What was Frances Lowe's reaction to the events?   *(4 marks)*

Now read **Source 2**, the leaflet called *Be Safe In Your Own Home* and answer the question below.

3. What message is the leaflet putting across about the importance of safety in the home?   *(8 marks)*

Now read **Source 3**, the web page headed *Now Health and Safety Really Have Gone Mad!* and answer the question below.

4. How does the writer use language to **argue** that health and safety rules are too strict?   *(12 marks)*

Now look again at all three sources. Choose **two** of these sources and compare the **presentational features**.

5. I have chosen source… and source…

   Remember to:
   - Write about the way the sources are presented
   - Compare how they look.   *(12 marks)*

Source 1

MY HOUSE FELL OFF A CLIFF!

One woman's anguish as she saw her life disappear

By Frances Lowe

I stood helplessly, clinging to my husband Ron, and watched as our life savings – almost our whole life – went hurtling down the cliff face. That bungalow meant everything to us and now it was gone.

EROSION

The cause of it was coastal erosion, the result of the constant beating of tidal waves against the cliffs. It's been going on for centuries with whole villages disappearing in East Anglia. I've also learned that attempts to shore up the cliffs often make things worse. You can't fight the power of nature.

ALARM BELLS

When we bought the bungalow, some thirty years ago we must have been 500 yards from the cliff edge and nobody mentioned erosion. We just fell in love with the glorious views over the North Sea. It did seem as if the sea was getting a little closer year by year, but it was such a gradual process. I suppose alarm bells should have rung when we found that it was becoming harder and harder to get insurance.

AUSTRALIA

Last year, to celebrate our wedding anniversary, we went on the trip of a lifetime. We took a whole six months to visit our grown up children, Justin and Lizzie, and their families in Australia and New Zealand. We had the time of our lives and didn't give a second thought to what was going on in England.

SHOCK

Imagine how we felt when, drowsy with jet lag but looking forward to getting home, we drove round the corner from the village and saw it... what was left of our bungalow. The area was cordoned off and both our house and the one next door looked as if a bomb had dropped on them. Our neighbours had packed up and gone. The bungalow was actually moving in front of our eyes. It was too late to save anything, but not too late to watch in horror as all our worldly goods disappeared into the North Sea.

BE SAFE IN YOUR OWN HOME

Home is where the heart is and it's a place where we should all feel safe – especially when we're not as young as we used to be. But did you know that 80% of all accidents dealt with in the A&E departments of our hospitals happen in the home? It's so easy to avoid accidents with just a little bit of care and foresight. We've put together a few handy hints to help you.

1 SLIPS AND TRIPS

It's amazing how many serious accidents are a result of slips and trips. To help avoid them:
*   Make sure all mats and carpets are secure.
*   Clean up spillages straight away.
*   Wear slippers with a good grip – don't walk round in your socks!

2 FALLS

Heights are dangerous but we can't always avoid them:
*   If climbing a ladder make sure there's someone there to keep it steady.
*   Don't stand on stools or chairs to do jobs like changing light bulbs.
*   Always hold on to safety rails when climbing stairs or getting in and out of the bath.

3 FIRE

Fire is the number one hazard in British homes:
*   Switch off all electrical appliances before going to bed.
*   Don't leave candles burning when you leave a room.
*   Make sure you've got a smoke alarm that's in working order.
*   Get a fire blanket to keep in the kitchen.

If you'd like more advice or help with implementing this advice, please call us now on 0708-952-66356 or visit our website: www.safetyinthehome.org.co.uk

 Remember – be safe, not sorry! The British Council for Safety in the Home

HOME | NEWS | GUIDANCE | ABOUT YOU | CONTACT US

NOW HEALTH AND SAFETY REALLY HAVE GONE MAD!
by Andrew Stringer

It's become such a cliché, hasn't it? Health and Safety gone mad! Yes, I appreciate that there is a need for some rules and regulations. We need to be healthy. We need to be safe. And sometimes we need a little help with that. But after what I've experienced in the last few weeks, I'm beginning to think health and safety really have gone mad.

First, I got involved in the whole 'Healthy Schools' business. No, it's not just something the *Coronation Street* writers made up. It's really happening in schools all over the country. Including my daughter's. Phoebe's seven. She came home in tears one day last week because a dinner lady had stolen her sweets! This harridan is paid to stand guard at the entrance to the school canteen and inspect the children's lunch boxes as they enter. If there's anything in there that appears on the list of forbidden foods – sweets, biscuits, sausage rolls – she confiscates it. I kid you not. And it seems the head teacher is right behind her, the governors are right behind her and the government is right behind them. It's called the 'Healthy School Initiative' or some such thing.

Well, I'm sorry, but we're her parents. We are responsible for seeing that she is fit and healthy. And that includes a balanced diet. We also happen to believe that the occasional treat is not going to ruin her health. What our daughter eats should be our decision, not the Health Fascists'.

And then there's the business of banning footballs in the playground. No, you heard right, footballs are forbidden in playgrounds! Apparently the head teacher of a primary school just down the road from us has banned the children from playing football in his school. Why? Because the balls might 'injure the children'.

So on the one hand, the government's telling us we've all got to do more sport to keep fit, while on the other their minions, like this crazed head teacher (who obviously hasn't got any real work to do) ban our children from playing the national game.

You might think these are isolated cases but I've heard of many more and, if you ask me, it's time we put the brakes on. Are Health and Safety important? Of course they are. But let's use a little common sense and put a bit more trust in people's ability to make their own decisions.

What do you think? Join the debate by clicking on the link below.

Have your say

Exam Practice Questions: Higher Tier

Section A of the Higher Tier exam will consist of four questions: 1, 2, 3 and 4. Here are examples of
these questions.
- *Answer all the questions.*
- *You are advised to spend 1 hour 15 minutes on these questions.*

Read **Source 1**, the website article called *Daffodils*, and answer the question below.

1. What do you learn about daffodils from this article? *(8 marks)*

Now read **Source 2**, the web page from the Marie Curie Cancer Care website, and answer the
question below.

2. Explain how the web page uses presentational devices to help persuade people to give to
the charity. *(8 marks)*

Now read **Source 3**, the extract from Dorothy Wordsworth's Diary for 15th April 1802,
and answer the question below.

3. Explain how Dorothy Wordsworth feels about her walk and how she reacts to the sight
of the daffodils. *(8 marks)*

Refer to **Source 3** again, the extract from Dorothy Wordsworth's diary, and **either Source 1
or Source 2**. You are going to compare the **two** texts, one of which you have chosen.

4. Compare the different ways in which language is used for effect in the two texts.
Give examples and analyse what the effects are. *(16 marks)*

Daffodils

home | news | shop online | about us | contact us

We all love daffodils, don't we? These iconic flowers have come to symbolise everything we associate with the coming of spring - hope, joy, beauty and even re-birth.

Did you know?

The earliest known references to daffodils date from about 300 BC. Their ancestors grew all around the Mediterranean, in present day Spain and Portugal as well as the Middle East. The Greeks and Romans grew daffodils and the Romans, who mistakenly thought they had healing powers, brought them to Britain.

Later the daffodil fell out of favour with the British and came to be seen as a weed until, in the early 17th century, some gardeners in England starting planting daffs in their gardens again. Since then they have become big business in Britain with tens of thousands bought every spring, especially for Mother's Day and Easter Sunday.

All about the daff

Daffodils are perennials, growing from bulbs. They grow best in climates that have cold winters and cool springs. They flower early in the spring in temperate climates, typically appearing in Britain in early March. Flowers can be single or double. There can be just one or several on a stem, which can be anything from six to twenty inches high.

They often grow in large groups, covering lawns and hillsides. It is not unusual to see, as the poet Wordsworth did, 'a host of golden daffodils' brightening up the British landscape in springtime.

How to Plant Them and Care for Them

- Plant them in Autumn

- Plant them at a depth of about three times the bulb's height (anything from 2 to 8 inches)

- Set the bulb in the soil pointy end up

- Avoid high-nitrogen fertilisers

- Make sure they have plenty of water

Follow this advice and next spring you could have your own 'host of golden daffodils... fluttering and dancing in the breeze'!

If you have any questions, don't hesitate to get in touch with our experts by clicking the link below.

Get in touch

Source 2

Thursday 15th April 1802

It was a threatening, misty morning, but mild. We set off after dinner from Eusemere. Mrs Clarkson went a short way with us, but turned back. The wind was furious and we thought we must have returned. We first rested in the large boat-house, then under a furze bush opposite Mr Clarkson's. Saw the plough going into the field. The wind seized our breath. The lake was rough. There was a boat by itself floating in the middle of the bay below Water Millock. We rested again in the Water Millock Lane. The hawthornes are black and green, the birches here and there greenish, but there is yet more of purple to be seen on the twigs. We got over into a field to avoid some cows - people working. A few primroses by the roadside - woodsorrel flower, the anemone, scentless violets, strawberries, and that starry yellow flower which Mrs C. calls pile wort. When we were in the woods beyond Gowbarrow Park we saw a few daffodils close to the water-side. We fancied that the lake had floated the seeds ashore, and that the little colony had so sprung up. But as we went along there were more and yet more; and at last, under the boughs of the trees, we saw that there was a long belt of them along the shore, about the breadth of a country turnpike road. I never saw daffodils so beautiful. They grew among the mossy stones about and about them; some rested their heads upon those stones as on a pillow for weariness; and the rest tossed and reeled and danced, and seemed as if they verily laughed with the wind, that blew upon them over the lake; they looked so gay, ever glancing, ever changing. This wind blew directly over the lake to them. There was here and there a little knot, and a few stragglers a few yards higher up; but they were so few as not to disturb the simplicity, unity, and life of that one busy highway.

The Writing Section of the Exam

The Exam Paper

Section B of the exam is the writing section. It contains **two** questions. You are not given a choice of questions: you must answer both questions. The answer to the second question is expected to be longer than the answer to the first question.

In the writing section, you're being tested on your ability to write non-fiction texts. This is sometimes referred to as **functional writing** because, unlike creative writing, it's the kind of writing you might need to do in everyday life.

Skills Assessed in the Exam

You'll be assessed on your ability to:

- Communicate ideas to your reader.
- Engage and interest the reader.
- Clearly communicate the **purpose** of your writing.
- Write in the appropriate **register** for your **audience**.
- Use linguistic features appropriate to purpose.
- Use correct **spelling** and **punctuation**.

- Use effective **vocabulary**, including **discourse markers**.
- Write in proper **sentences**.
- Use **grammar** accurately.
- Use a variety of **sentence forms**.
- Use **Standard English** accurately.

These skills are covered in this revision guide.

What the Writing Exam Looks Like

It's a good idea to look ahead now to the Practice Exam Questions for Foundation Tier and Higher Tier on pages 86–87. As you read through this book, keep glancing at these to remind yourself of what the writing part of the exam is likely to consist of.

Genre and Form

Each question will ask you to write in a particular **genre** or **form**.

You'll already be familiar with different forms and will have learned how to read and analyse them. For the writing section, you need to be able to write in them.

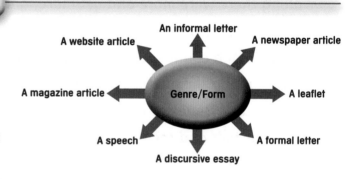

Purpose and Audience

The main **purposes** of non-fiction texts include:
- Writing to inform.
- Writing to explain.
- Writing to describe.
- Writing to argue.
- Writing to persuade.
- Writing to advise.

The exam question might ask you to write for any of these purposes. The question might also tell you who your **audience** is, for example:
- Fellow students.
- Younger pupils.
- The head teacher.
- Your MP or local councillor.

Time Management

You're advised to spend **one hour** completing the two writing tasks.

You should spend around **25 minutes** on the first task (worth 16 marks) and around **35 minutes** on the second (worth 24 marks). So your second answer should be longer and more detailed.

You don't have to stick exactly to this, but if you take much longer than 25 minutes on the first task, you may not be able to develop your second answer sufficiently to gain a high mark.

You'll also need to allow yourself a little time to plan each answer and to check each answer for errors.

Planning Your Answers

It's a good idea to make a quick plan before embarking on each task.

The first thing you should do is make sure that you're clear on:

- The **purpose** of your writing.
- The **audience** for whom you are writing.
- The **genre** or **form** in which you'll be writing.

Your plan will not be marked but you should do it in your answer book. Different people plan in different ways. Some of the most popular planning techniques include:

- Mind maps/spider diagrams.
- Bullet points/lists.
- Flow charts.
- Writing frames.

Whichever method you use, make sure you put your ideas in a logical order. Don't spend longer than five minutes on your plan.

LETTER TO GOVERNORS

Paragraph 1: Uniform is bad
- Everyone looks the same
- Ties are dangerous
- Uncomfortable

Paragraph 2: Uniform is good
- Looks tidy
- Poorer pupils can afford it
- Makes you feel part of school

Paragraph 3: Why the above is wrong
- Everyone tries to make it look different
- Still know who the poor kids are
- Shouldn't need uniform to make you feel like you belong

Conclusion
- Europe does not have uniform
- This is the 21st century – people can be more individual

Paragraph 1 Why uniform is bad - Everyone looks the same - Ties are dangerous - Uncomfortable	Paragraph 2 Why uniform is good - Looks tidy - Poorer pupils can afford it - Makes you feel part of school
LETTER TO GOVERNORS	
Paragraph 3 Why the above is wrong - Everyone tries to make it look different - Everyone still knows who the poor kids are - Shouldn't need uniform to make you feel like you belong	Conclusion - Europe does not have uniform - This is the 21st century – people can be more individual

Date

Address

Dear

On behalf of the school council, I am writing...

We feel very strongly about this issue.

Although I recognise that there are some arguments against my proposals...

However I feel that...

I hope, therefore, that you can offer your support...

Yours...

Checking Your Answers

You should spend a few minutes checking your answers.

Check that:

- You've answered both questions.
- You've used the correct **form** for each question.
- You've written in clear **paragraphs**.
- Your paragraphs are linked using **connectives**.
- Your **punctuation** is correct.

- Your **spelling** – especially of easily confused words – is correct.
- You've used correct **grammar** and have written in **Standard English**.

If you find a mistake, cross it out neatly and make the correction clearly. You will not be penalised for having made errors which you have then corrected.

Punctuation

Punctuation Marks

To achieve a grade C you're expected to be using full stops, question marks and commas correctly and to be able to punctuate direct speech.

To achieve a grade A you'll need to use a range of punctuation accurately. This might include ellipsis, colons and semi-colons.

Full Stops

Full stops separate sentences. A common mistake students make is to use commas instead of full stops.

Question Marks

Question marks come at the end of questions.
- They can be used in direct speech:
  - *'What is really going on?' asked the leader.*
- They can be used at the end of normal and rhetorical questions:
  - *Do you really want to see your local environment destroyed?*

Exclamation Marks

Exclamation marks act like full stops, but they're used to show surprise, shock, enthusiasm and other extreme emotions:
  - *Stand up for your rights now!*

Use exclamation marks sparingly. If you use too many, they stop being effective.

Commas

1. **Commas** mark smaller breaks or pauses than full stops. They mustn't be used to link two statements that could stand alone as sentences (**clauses**) unless a **connective** or **relative pronoun** is used:
   - *I fed the dog, although it had eaten.*
   - *I fed the dog, which was very friendly.*
2. Commas separate **subordinate clauses** from **main clauses**. Subordinate clauses give extra information but aren't necessary for the sentence to make sense:
   - *Antony, having run fast, was exhausted.*
3. Commas are also used to list items:
   - *I bought sugar, flour, beans and a candle.*
4. Commas introduce and end direct speech:
   - *He was shouting, 'Get me out of here!'*
   - *'Nobody move,' ordered the policeman.*

Colons

1. **Colons** are used before an explanation:
   - *It took all day: only two men were working.*
2. Colons introduce quotations:
   - *Mercutio plays down his injury: 'Ay, ay, a scratch, a scratch'.*
3. Colons often introduce lists:
   - *The collection was varied: historic manuscripts; ancient bones; and hundreds of coins.*

Semi-colons

1. **Semi-colons** show that two clauses are related:
   - *The flowers are blooming; the trees are green.*
2. Semi-colons separate items in a list that are more than one word:
   - *The collection was varied: historic manuscripts; ancient bones; and hundreds of coins.*

Parentheses (Brackets)

Parentheses or brackets are placed around extra information, sometimes an explanation, which has been placed in a sentence:
- *A huge man (who was seven foot tall) sat watching.*

Dashes

Dashes are similar to brackets, indicating an interruption in the train of thought:
- *I went to the restaurant – if you could call it that – and ordered a drink.*

Key Words Full stop • Question mark • Comma • Colon • Semi-colon • Exclamation mark • Parentheses

Punctuation Marks (Cont.)

Ellipsis

Ellipsis means the omission of words from a sentence and is shown by three dots. It's often used to show a thought trailing off or to make the reader wonder what comes next:

- *I suddenly realised I wasn't alone…*

Inverted Commas

Inverted commas are referred to as **speech marks** or **quotation marks**, according to their function:

- **Speech marks** surround the words spoken:
  - *'I never want to see you again!' he cried.*
- **Quotation marks** show words from a text:
  - *Tybalt refers to Romeo as 'that villain'.*

Apostrophes

Apostrophes are easy to use if you remember that there are only **two reasons** for using them:

- To show **omission** (also referred to as **contraction**), i.e. leaving out letters.
- To show **possession** (belonging).

Apostrophes for Omission

You only need apostrophes for omission when writing **informally**.

An apostrophe of omission shows where the missing letter or letters would have been:

- *You **shouldn't** have done that.*
- ***Mark's** finished but **Rachel's** still working.*

Apostrophes for Possession

Apostrophes are used to show possession:

- If the owner is singular, add an apostrophe and an 's' to the word that indicates the 'owner':
  - *The **cat's** tail* (the tail of the cat).
  - *The **class's** teacher* (the teacher of the class).
- If the word for more than one owner doesn't end in 's', you still add an apostrophe and 's' to the word that indicates the owner:
  - *The **children's** toys* (the toys belong to more than one child – the children).
  - *The **men's** championship* (one championship but more than one man).
- When the word indicating the plural owners ends in 's', simply add an apostrophe after 's':
  - *The **cats'** tails* (the tails of the cats).
  - *The **boys'** book* (the book of the boys – there are several boys but they only have one book).

Quick Test

1. Insert the correct punctuation:
   a) The dog had disappeared there was no doubt about that
   b) Wheres my dog she cried bring him back
   c) The dogs owner was not happy however when it jumped on the stage
   d) The magician who was remarkably tall and fat acknowledged the audiences applause

Sentence Forms

To get a good grade at GCSE, you're expected to know when to start a new sentence, to start each sentence with a **capital letter** and to end it with a **full stop**.

For the higher grades, you're expected to vary your **sentence forms**. Sentences should vary in length and be properly constructed. There are four main forms:

- **Simple sentences**.
- **Compound sentences**.
- **Complex sentences**.
- **Minor sentences** or **fragments**.

Simple Sentences

Every sentence must contain a **subject** and a **main verb**. The subject is the person or thing (a **noun**) that the sentence is about. The verb is the doing, feeling or being word. For example:

- *Dan sleeps.*

> **Subject** **Verb**

Simple sentences often include an **object** (a **noun**). For example:

- *Syed ate the apple.*

> **Subject** **Verb** **Object**

Simple sentences may also include a **preposition**, which explains the subject's relationship to the object:

- *Chloe slept on the bed.*

> **Subject** **Verb** **Preposition** **Object**

Active and Passive

You can vary simple sentences, and other sentence forms, by changing the verb from **active** to **passive**:

- *The apple was eaten by Syed.*

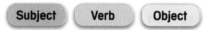

> **Subject** **Verb** **Object**

Here the apple, not Syed, is the subject of the sentence and, by being put at the start of the sentence, becomes more important.

Compound Sentences

To make a **compound sentence** you join together **two clauses** (phrases that could stand alone as simple sentences) using a **conjunction**:

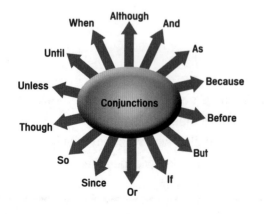

The conjunction tells you what the relationship is between the two clauses. For example:

- *Maria left the room **and** went to the shop.*
- *Maria left the room **but** stayed in the house.*
- *Maria left the room **because** she wanted to go to the shop.*

Sometimes the conjunction is placed at the beginning of the sentence rather than between the two clauses, for example:

- ***Although** he felt ill, Syed ate an apple.*
- ***Because** she felt ill, Chloe went to bed.*
- ***Until** she went to bed, Chloe felt ill.*

Complex Sentences

Like a compound sentence, a **complex sentence** also has two or more clauses joined together.

The **main clause** should make sense on its own but the **subordinate clause**, which adds detail or explanation, doesn't need to make sense on its own.

Conjunctions aren't needed to form complex sentences; instead, **subordinate clauses** are placed between commas. For example:

- *Maria, who loved shopping, left the house immediately.*

The subordinate clause in this example is 'who loved shopping'.

This example uses a **relative pronoun** ('who') to connect the clauses.

The subordinate clause can be placed at the beginning or end of the main clause, before or after a comma. For example:

- *Having left the house quickly, Maria went shopping.*
- *Maria went shopping, having left the house quickly.*

These examples change the verb form to a **participle** 'having left' to connect the clauses.

You can build even longer sentences by using several clauses and joining them in an appropriate way. For example:

- *Maria, having discovered that there was no food left, decided to go shopping and left the house.*
- *Chloe was ill for several days so she stayed in bed, sometimes reading and sometimes watching television, but mostly just being bored and grumpy.*

Minor Sentences

A **minor sentence**, also known as a **fragment**, isn't really a sentence at all because it doesn't contain a main verb.

Minor sentences are very short and are used for effect, for example in persuasive writing. They're often answers to questions or exclamations. For example:

- *On my word!*
- *Just another boring day.*

They shouldn't be used too often or they lose their impact.

Quick Test

1. Decide whether each of the following is a simple sentence, a compound sentence, a complex sentence or a minor sentence.
   a) She was twenty-five but she seemed older.
   b) Never in a million years.
   c) The room was quite silent.
   d) The streets, throbbing with humanity, were frightening to a child who had grown up in the countryside.

Spelling

Why Spelling Matters

Correct **spelling** matters because readers need to understand what you're trying to say.

Some English spellings can be difficult and the examiners don't expect you to get every word right.

But, to get a grade C you're expected to spell most words correctly. To get a grade A you must also be able to correctly spell less commonly used words, which may not follow regular spelling patterns.

Spelling Rules

Nouns and Verbs Ending in 'y'

Some **nouns** end in a **consonant** and '**y**'. When you make these nouns **plural** by adding 's', the 'y' becomes '**ie**': Diary → Diaries

Some nouns end in a **vowel** and 'y'. To make these nouns **plural**, just add 's': Boy → Boys

For **verbs** ending in 'y', follow the same rule:
Vary → Varies

A similar rule applies when you add 'ed' to put a **verb** in the **past tense**:
Pity → Pitied

Note that 'say' becomes 'said', not 'sayed' as you might expect. That's the trouble with spelling rules – there are usually exceptions!

'I' before 'e' except after 'c'

"I' before 'e' except after 'c" applies to 'ee' sounds like in these words: achieve, believe, ceiling, receive.

Spelling Strategies

Mnemonics are ways of remembering things.

Some people find it useful to have a phrase where the first letters of the words spell out the word you're trying to spell, for example:

- **B**ig **e**lephants **c**an **a**lways **u**pset **s**mall **e**lephants = **because**

You might associate the spelling with a memorable phrase, for example:

- Ne**cess**ary – one collar, two socks.

Or you might isolate the tricky part of the word:

- There's **a rat** in sep**arat**e.

Over-pronouncing (i.e. splitting the word up and saying it carefully) can help, for example:

- En–vir–on–**m**ent
- **K**–now–le**d**–ge

Whatever strategies you use to learn spellings, the important thing is that you identify the ones you tend to get wrong. Make a list of them and set about learning them.

Noun • Consonant • Plural • Vowel • Verb

Homophones

Homophones are words that sound the same but have different meanings. For example:

Here means 'in this place': *'It's over here'.*
You **hear** with your ears: *'I can hear you'.*

There means 'in that place': *I put it over there.'* It's also used in phrases such as *'there is'* and *'there are'.*
They're is a contraction of 'they are': *'They're not really friends'.*
Their means 'belonging to them': *'They took all their things with them'.*

Where, like 'here' and 'there', refers to place: *'Where do you think you're going?'*
We're is a contraction of 'we are': *'We're going to pass the exam'.*
Wear refers to clothes, etc.: *'You wear your earrings on your ears'.* It's also used in the sense of 'wearing' something out.
Were is part of the verb 'to be', the past tense of are: *'We were very happy.'; 'If I were in charge, there would be big changes'.*

To indicates direction: *'He went to the cinema'.* It's also used as part of a verb: *'I want to do this now'.*
Too means excessively: *'Too much'* or *'Too many'.* It can also mean 'as well': *'She ate my sweets too'.*
Two is the number 2: *'There were two questions'.*

Accept means to receive: *'I accept your gift'.*
Except means apart from: *'I like them all, except the green one'.*

Affect is a verb: *'This decision affects us all'.*
Effect is a noun: *'The effects are terrible'.*

Aloud is the same as 'out loud': *'I will read aloud'.*
Allowed means permitted: *'Chewing gum is not allowed in school'.*

Its means 'belonging to it': *'The dog wagged its tail'.*
It's is a contraction of 'it is': *'It's mine'.*

Know is to be aware: *'I know who he is'.*
No is the opposite of yes.

Knew is the past tense of know: *'I knew who it was'.*
New is the opposite of old: *'I bought a new dress'.*

Passed is the past tense of the verb 'pass': *'I passed all my exams'.*
Past indicates a previous time: *'It's all in the past'.* It's also used in phrases like *'he walked past'* and *'it's past its best'.*

Practice is a noun: *'She's late for netball practice'.*
Practise is a verb: *'You must practise every day to get better.'* (The same rule applies to advice/advise and licence/license.)

Right is the opposite of wrong: *'I got it right!'*
Write is what you do in an exam: *'Write an essay'.*

Weather refers to the sun, rain etc.: *'The weather's been terrible today'.*
Whether is similar to 'if': *'I don't know whether to go out or not'.*

Who's is a contraction of 'who is': *'Who's that?'*
Whose means 'belonging to whom': *'Whose coat is it?'*

Your means 'belonging to you': *'It's your book'.*
You're is a contraction of 'you are': *'You're beautiful'.*

Quick Test

1. Identify the correct spelling from the alternatives given in the following sentences:

   a) I can't go out because I have to **practice/practise** my song.

   b) We had no idea **were/where** we **were/where** going.

   c) **Its/It's** Saturday tomorrow.

   d) I can't decide **weather/whether** to take the bus or the train.

Standard English and Grammar

Standard English

Standard English is the most widely accepted **dialect** of English. A **dialect** is a variation of a language, which has its own vocabulary and grammatical forms. Dialect shouldn't be confused with **accent**, which is how people pronounce words.

A dialect may be associated with a part of the country. Different dialects used to mean that people from one part of the country didn't understand people from another so 'Standard English' became the version of English to be used in formal writing.

You should be aware of any words or phrases which are common in your area but aren't Standard English. Avoid using them in formal writing.

Avoid using slang ('sick' for 'good' and double negatives like 'I haven't got nothing') and Americanisms ('gotten' for 'got') unless appropriate.

The examiners want to see that you can write in Standard English so at least one of the writing questions will demand that you use it.

But for one of the questions you might not need to write entirely in Standard English. For example:
- If you want to use direct speech, quoting from someone who doesn't use Standard English.
- If you're asked to write for an audience of teenagers or children.

In these cases, **non-standard English** is desirable.

Personal Pronouns

First Person

The most common misuse of **personal pronouns** is the confusion of 'I' and 'me'. 'I' is the **subject** of the sentence; 'me' is the **object**:
- Ikram and **me** missed the first lesson. ✗

This is wrong because you wouldn't say: 'Me missed the first lesson'. You'd say: 'I missed the first lesson'. So, it must be:
- Ikram and **I** missed the first lesson. ✓

Similarly, you shouldn't say:
- They gave prizes to Lucy and **I**. ✗

This is wrong because you wouldn't say 'They gave a prize to I'. You'd say: 'They gave a prize to me'. So the correct form is:
- They gave prizes to Lucy and **me**. ✓

Second Person

'You' refers to either one person or many. If you want to make it clear that you're speaking to more than one person, you could say something like 'Thank you all for coming'.

Avoid using the Americanism, 'you guys'. This isn't Standard English.

Modal Verbs

A common error among pupils is the use of the word 'of' instead of 'have' after **modal verbs** such as 'would', 'could' and 'might'.

You must use 'have':
- If I'd known, I would **have** told you.
- You should **have** got an earlier bus.

Verbs: Agreement

Verb agreement means using the correct form of a **verb** with a **personal pronoun**. Errors in this area are common, especially with the irregular verb 'to be':

	Singular	Plural
Present tense	I am, You are, He/She/It is	We are, You are, They are
(Simple) Past tense	I was, You were, He/She/It was	We were, You were, They were

Most verbs are regular and follow this pattern:

	Singular	Plural
Present tense	I/You walk, He/She/It walks	We/You walk, They walk
(Simple) Past tense	I/You walked, He/She/It walked	We walked, You/They walked

Verbs: Control of Tenses

The **perfect tense** expresses a completed action and is formed using 'has'/'have' and the **past participle**. For example:

- I **walk** to school. (**Present tense**)
- I **walked** to school. (**Simple past tense**)
- I **have walked** to school. (**Perfect tense**)

This table shows the correct forms for some of the most common irregular verbs:

Present	Simple Past	Perfect
am/is are	was were	have been has been
do does	did	have done has done

Present	Simple Past	Perfect
eat eats	ate	have eaten has eaten
get gets	got	have got has got
give gives	gave	have given has given
go goes	went	have gone has gone
lie lies	lay	have lain has lain
see sees	saw	have seen has seen
sing sings	sang	have sung has sung

Other Forms of the Past Tense

The **imperfect tense** expresses a past action, which might not have been completed. It's formed using 'was'/'were' and the **present participle**. For example:

- I was walking to school.
- We were playing when he arrived.

If you're writing in the past tense and want to refer to something that happened before, use the **past perfect tense** (pluperfect), which is formed by using 'had' and the **past participle**:

- By the time I arrived, I **had walked** five miles.
- After he **had eaten** six apples he felt sick.

Quick Test

1 Write each of these sentences out in Standard English.
   a) Me and Jay was put on detention.
   b) I seen you guys on Saturday.
   c) You was the best player we had.
   d) We'd sang the first one, so afterwards we done a dance.

Paragraphs

What are Paragraphs?

Paragraphs organise writing so that it makes sense, follows a logical order and is easier to read. To gain a grade C you're expected to use paragraphs. For a grade A you're expected to use paragraphs **effectively**.

A new paragraph can be shown by:
- Leaving a line between the new paragraph and the previous one.
- **Indenting** the first line of the new paragraph – examiners prefer to see indentation.

For example:

> The problem has become worse over the last few months. Yesterday I saw two foxes raiding the bins in my own front garden and I know a number of neighbours have had the same problem.
>
> As a result of this, we are concerned not only about our pets, but also about our children. These animals spread diseases.

When to Start a New Paragraph

- **Change of speaker** – when writing direct speech, always start a new paragraph when a new person starts to speak:

> 'When we left, there was nobody else on the boat,' added Charlie Higgs.

- **Change of person** – you might be introducing a new person who hasn't been mentioned yet:

> Laurie Grantham, 17, has a very different attitude to fashion.

- **Change of place**:

> On the other side of the park, the lions roam free.

- **Change of time**:

> Some months later, Ronald realised that all was not well.

- **Change of topic/idea** – you might be moving from one aspect of your subject to another:

> Another area of concern is the state of the local playground.

Or you could be introducing a new, different opinion about the topic.

> Some residents disagree with this view, however.

There is no set length for paragraphs.

Topic Sentences

The first sentence of a paragraph is a **topic sentence**: it introduces the new topic that the paragraph will be about.

> 'When we left, there was nobody else on the boat,' added Charlie Higgs.

This topic sentence tells us that this paragraph will be about the boat and whether or not it was empty.

> Laurie Grantham, 17, has a very different attitude to fashion.

Reading this topic sentence, we'd expect to find out what ideas Laurie Grantham has about fashion and how they differ from those discussed in the previous paragraph.

Effective Opening Paragraphs

A good opening paragraph should make your **intention** clear to the readers and gain their attention.

For example, a formal letter usually starts by stating what the letter is about in a simple but **polite** way:

> I am writing to express my concern about the deteriorating environment around St. Mungo's Shopping Centre. I have lived in this area for many years and used to find shopping at St. Mungo's a very pleasant experience. Recently, however, I have found myself dreading the experience.

This paragraph sets out clearly why the writer is writing the letter.

Articles often start with an **anecdote** to 'hook' the reader:

> The final straw came when I got to checkout. There was no-one there. I looked around and could see no-one resembling a shop assistant. Was this really one of Britain's best loved department stores on a Saturday afternoon?

This writer has used **personal experience** to draw in the reader.

Other forms, especially when their purpose is to persuade, might start by flattering the reader:

> You're a busy person. You've got responsibilities. There are more important things to worry about than the state of your drains. We understand that, which is why we're making you this fabulous offer.

This paragraph speaks directly to readers, making them feel important, before saying what it's about.

Effective Closing Paragraphs

A good concluding paragraph usually **summarises the main points** you've made. If you've discussed several points of view, you might end by saying which you agree with and why. Or, you could leave your readers with questions to think about. Read these examples:

> I am sure that you will agree with me that these problems need to be taken seriously. I urge you to raise this matter at your next meeting and press for action to be taken immediately.

> Not enough staff on the checkout; shop assistants chatting and a complete lack of old-fashioned courtesy. That's my experience of Britain's shops today. Let's stop being doormats and start insisting on good service.

> We do all these things and more. We're local, we're trustworthy and we're reliable. For a free home visit and estimate, call us now. Make blocked drains a thing of the past!

Quick Test

1. What is the best way to show paragraphs in the exam?
2. List two points in your writing when you would need to start a new paragraph.

Connecting Sentences and Paragraphs

Discourse Markers

Connectives, such as **conjunctions** and **relative pronouns** can be used to connect clauses in order to make longer sentences (see pages 50–51).

You also need to show that you can connect sentences and paragraphs effectively using **discourse markers** (**discursive markers**). Discourse markers help guide readers through the text, showing how sentences and paragraphs relate to each other.

You don't have to use a discourse marker every time you start a new paragraph or sentence. It's possible to connect paragraphs by picking up on an idea from the previous paragraph. For example:

> This kind of prejudice is common throughout Europe.

It's clear from this **topic sentence** that the previous paragraph was about prejudice, and the new paragraph is going to discuss its existence in different countries in Europe.

When you use discourse markers, it's essential that you know what they mean and how they connect the paragraphs.

Not all discourse markers have to be used at the beginning of a sentence. Some, such as 'However', can be more effective a little way into the sentence.

Types of Discourse Markers

Discourse markers can be used for various purposes, as shown here:

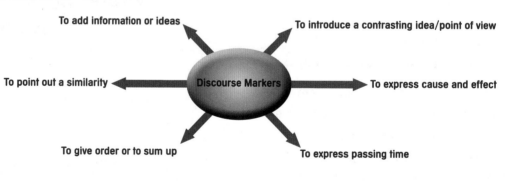

- To add information or ideas
- To introduce a contrasting idea/point of view
- To point out a similarity
- Discourse Markers
- To express cause and effect
- To give order or to sum up
- To express passing time

To Add Information or Ideas – Examples

- **In addition**, the announcement is likely to cause mass panic.
- **As well as** showing he knows little about it, he has demonstrated that he doesn't care.
- **Furthermore**, students are unable to concentrate in class after staying out late.
- The new building, **moreover**, will block out the light from existing houses.

To Express Cause and Effect – Examples

- I have had no response. I have decided, **therefore**, to withdraw my offer.
- **As a result**, I have decided to resign.
- **Consequently**, I've decided to go ahead.
- **In order to** raise her profile, Antonia made sure she spoke at every meeting.
- **Inevitably**, this led to disappointment.
- **Due to** the cold weather, gas bills have risen.

Connecting Sentences and Paragraphs

Types of Discourse Markers (Cont.)

To Introduce a Contrasting Idea – Examples

- Many good points have been made in favour. **Nevertheless**, I think it's a bad idea.
- Harry made excellent progress. Joe, **on the other hand**, seemed to go backwards.
- **In spite of** all the obstacles in our path, I still think we can win this election.
- **In contrast to** Jenny's optimism, Laura is convinced the plans will be rejected.
- Washington is a beautiful city. New York, **however**, is most people's favourite.
- **Alternatively**, you might be interested in one of our luxury holidays.

To Express Passing Time – Examples

- They left early. **Subsequently**, they disappeared.
- **Later** we realised what had happened.
- **Before** this unfortunate incident, nobody had even heard of Archie Wainwright.
- **Previously**, most people thought the world was flat.
- I saw her on the other side of the street. **Immediately** I ran over to her.
- **The following** night it happened again.
- **As soon as** I realised what was going on, I phoned the police.
- The police took an hour to arrive. **Meanwhile**, Archie had escaped.

To Give Order or to Sum Up – Examples

- **Firstly**, I'd like to thank you for coming.
- **Finally**, I'd like to pay tribute to Josh and Leanna for making all this possible.
- **In conclusion**, I have no doubt that cats make better pets than dogs.
- **Overall**, this is a very innovative idea.
- **Essentially**, there are two sides to this story.
- **Basically**, it's about what we want.
- **In summary**, the advantages of this scheme outweigh the disadvantages.

To Point Out a Similarity – Examples

- **Similarly**, Year 8 pupils showed a preference for a shorter lunch break.
- **In the same way**, the owl hunts at night.

Quick Test

1. Identify the discourse markers in the following sentences and explain their purpose.
   a) Basically, nobody likes the idea.
   b) Carl's idea, on the other hand, is worthwhile.
   c) Before the car park was built, there were several species of butterfly here.
   d) I'd like, therefore, to propose we knock down the car park.

Purpose and Audience

Understanding Purpose and Audience

Writers usually write for a **purpose** and often have a target **audience** in mind. So, when you're the writer, you must always be aware of audience and purpose.

Audience

The tasks you're given in the exam often include the identity of the target audience.

It's essential that you correctly identify the audience before deciding what you're going to write and how you're going to write it.

When thinking about your audience you might ask:
1. Do I know the person/people?
2. How old are they?
3. What do I have in common with them?
4. What are they interested in?
5. What response am I trying to get?

Examples

Look at the example exam questions in the table. Then look at how you might identify your audience by asking yourself the questions above.

Write a letter to a local celebrity persuading him or her to support a fun run in aid of charity.	Write an article for a teenage magazine arguing the case for or against abolishing exams.
1. No, but I know a lot about him. 2. Probably in his twenties. 3. Our desire to raise money for this charity, sport and the local area. 4. The charity (I hope), sport and his career. 5. I want him to come to the school and start the fun run, helping us to make money.	1. No, I don't know the readers. 2. They're about my age. 3. We're the same age and they might be taking exams as well. We read the same magazine. 4. School will be important to them. They're probably into music, TV, fashion and sport. 5. I'd like to get them thinking about the issue and respond to the article, agreeing or disagreeing.

Purpose

The task will also tell you what the purpose of your writing is. For example:

Write a letter to a local celebrity persuading him or her to support a fun run in aid of charity.

Your purpose here is to **persuade** the celebrity to support you.

Write an article for a teenage magazine arguing the case for or against abolishing exams.

The key word here is '**arguing**'. This task allows you to decide whether you are 'for' or 'against'. Other tasks might tell you which side to argue.

Purpose and Audience

Appropriate Language

To get a good grade at GCSE, you're expected to write in a **register** which is **appropriate for the audience**. Register refers to the kind of language which is used, including whether it's **formal** or **informal**.

You're also expected to use **linguistic features appropriate to purpose**.

Informal Language and Register

If, having worked out your audience and purpose, you've decided that an informal tone is appropriate, (e.g. if writing for people of your own age) you might:

- Address your readers directly, using the **second person** ('you') and the **first person** ('I' or 'we') to show that you identify with them and their interests.
- Use abbreviations and **contractions**, e.g. 'you've'.

- Use the kind of **vocabulary** you use when talking to your friends. But don't overdo it and think carefully before using 'text language'.
- Use **alliteration**, **similes**, **metaphors** and even **rhyme** to achieve a lively tone.
- Refer to things that teenagers will identify with but adults might not, such as certain TV shows, celebrities, films and music.

Formal Language and Register

An older audience, like your teachers or the readers of a newspaper, probably wouldn't appreciate an informal tone and might not take you seriously if you use one. To achieve a more formal tone, you should:

- Use the **second person**, but not as often or in such a familiar way as in informal writing, e.g. 'You might be interested to know…' rather than 'Did you know that…?'
- Use **full words**, not contractions.
- **Avoid** slang – these people aren't your friends.

- Use a range of **punctuation**, but avoid exclamation marks and dashes.
- Use **complex sentences**.
- Use the **passive voice**, e.g. 'Many people were injured in the storm'.
- Be **polite**, using phrases such as 'I should be grateful if you would…'.
- Consider using **specialised language** if you know it, assuming the audience will understand it.

Quick Test

1 Decide whether each of these tasks is likely to require an informal tone or a formal tone.
   a) A letter to a friend asking her to visit.
   b) A letter to the Prime Minister giving your views on global warming.
   c) An article for a newspaper about unemployment among young people.
   d) A speech to an audience of teenagers about raising money for a charity.

Writing Informal Letters

Audience and Purpose

An **informal letter** is usually to a friend or relative – someone you know well and who knows you well. Informal letters are rarer than they used to be but many people write **e-mails** to friends and family.

You might also write an informal letter or e-mail to a magazine, especially one whose own style is chatty and friendly.

There are many reasons for writing an informal letter, including:

- Inviting someone to visit you.
- Thanking someone for a present.
- Telling someone that you've moved house.
- Simply putting down your thoughts on paper and sharing them with a friend.

Organisation and Presentation

There are some conventions that apply to both formal and informal letters:

- Write your address in the top right-hand corner of the page. This is important if you want a reply! (You could also put your telephone number and e-mail address under the address).
- Write the date (e.g. 5th June 2012, 5/6/12, Wednesday, 5th June) under your address, leaving a line in between.
- Begin your letter with 'Dear' followed by the person's name and a comma. This is called the **salutation**. If you're very close to the person you're writing to, you could start with another greeting.

- Leave a line after the salutation and begin the first paragraph by indenting.
- You can sign off in any way that seems appropriate, depending on your relationship, e.g. Love, Yours, followed by your first name (or the name the **recipient** calls you).

Some people like to put a PS (**post script**) after the signature, with something they perhaps forgot to put in the main body of the letter. This can give a sense of spontaneity appropriate to an informal letter. (It should never be done in a **formal** letter.)

E-mails

Many people **e-mail** friends and relatives. E-mails generally use the same kind of **language** and **tone** as a traditional letter, but they have their own conventions:

- You don't put your address at the top.
- You don't need to put the date.

A lot of people use abbreviations in e-mails, as they would when writing a text message. Some people like to insert **emoticons** or other **images**.

Language

An **informal** letter is, of course, written in an **informal register**, but this could vary a lot depending on the **recipient** (the person you're writing to) and the **purpose** of the letter.

Informal • Salutation • Recipient • Post script • Formal • Emoticon

Example Student Answer

This example is an informal letter written by a girl (Sadie) to her grandmother. It is written in a **register** that is appropriate to the relationship. Think about how the letter would differ if it were addressed to a close friend or a friend from another country.

> 42 Waverley Gardens
> Puddington
> Sussex
>
> 6th July 2012
>
> Dear Nan,
>
> Thank you for your lovely present. I have already worn them and everyone says how cool they look. How did you know green was my favourite colour? I can't believe you knitted them yourself. I really wish I could do that. I've asked Mum to teach me and she says she will when she's got time – but I don't know when that will be.
>
> I had a fantastic birthday. I went go-karting with some friends from school – and Mum and Dad and the boys, of course. It was a bit hair-raising but really good fun. We couldn't get Dad away, he was like a big kid, trying to beat everyone and asking for a re-match whenever he lost!
>
> After that we came home for a ginormous Chinese takeaway (my favourite) and a couple of my friends slept over.
>
> It's such a shame you couldn't be there. We all missed you and we've decided to have another party as soon as you get back from Australia. So I get to have two birthdays!
>
> Hope you're still having a great time over there. What have you all been up to since I last heard from you? Give my love to Auntie Pam and the kids. And thanks again for the hat and gloves; I'm sending you a picture of me wearing them.
>
> Lots of love,
> Sadie

Commentary

- The letter begins in quite a **formal** way, but has a friendly and familiar **tone**.
- It is set out using proper letter conventions.
- **Contractions** are used, which produces an appropriate informal register.
- **Informal punctuation** (dashes, brackets and exclamation marks) gives a sense of the writer's mood.
- Non-standard **vocabulary** is used. But she doesn't overdo this as she's writing to an older person, who might not understand all the words she uses with her friends.
- **First person** ('I', 'we') and **second person** ('you', 'your') are used.
- A couple of **questions** are asked to encourage the recipient to reply.

If this letter were a thank you note written to a friend it might be quite different. As well as words and phrases used in their friendship group, there might be shared jokes and references to mutual interests. She might also use '**text language**' and conventions.

If Sadie were writing to a pen-friend from abroad, perhaps someone she'd never met, she would have to be more careful with her language. However good the pen-friend's English, he/she wouldn't know all the latest slang and might need some things explaining so it would be best to avoid jokes.

Quick Test

1. State whether each of the following is a formal letter or an informal letter:
   - a) A letter of complaint to a shop.
   - b) A letter to a friend about your holiday.
   - c) A letter to a teenage magazine giving your thoughts on a celebrity's fashion sense.
   - d) A letter to a national newspaper about student debt.

Writing Formal Letters

Audience and Purpose

There's a very good chance that you'll be asked to write a formal letter in your exam.

You write in a more formal style when writing to someone you've never met or someone with whom you have a formal relationship, e.g.:
- An employer or prospective employer.
- Your head teacher or governors.
- Your MP or local councillor.

- The editor of a newspaper.
- A commercial organisation, e.g. a bank or shop.

There are many reasons for writing formal letters, including:
- In response to a newspaper/magazine article.
- To make a complaint.
- To apply for a job.
- To express your opinion on an issue.

Organisation and Presentation

Some of the conventions for writing formal letters are the same as those for informal letters but there are some extra 'rules':
- Write your address in the top right hand corner with a line space between this and the date.
- Write the date under your address.
- Write the name and address of the recipient on the left-hand side of the page.
- Begin your letter with 'Dear', the person's name and a comma. If you know the person's name, use 'Mr X', 'Mrs Y', etc. If you don't know the name, use 'Dear Sir/Madam'.

- Leave a line after the salutation and begin the first paragraph by indenting. Your first paragraph should make clear the reason for your writing, e.g:
  - I am writing to apply for the job advertised...
- Continue with paragraphs that make further points, explaining your point of view or intentions.
- End with a paragraph that states what you'd like to happen next.
- If you've addressed the reader by name sign off with '**Yours sincerely**'. If you wrote 'Sir/Madam', use '**Yours faithfully**'.

The 'Five Cs'

When writing a formal letter, remember the five Cs:
- **Complete** – give enough detail and explain your points properly.
- **Concise** – don't 'ramble'. Don't include irrelevant information or ideas.
- **Correct** – your writing must make sense and be spelt and punctuated correctly.

- **Clear** – express yourself clearly so the reader knows exactly what you mean.
- **Courteous** – be polite. Consider the recipient's reactions to what you're saying. You're more likely to get a positive reaction if you're courteous.

Language

You should always use **Standard English**; avoid slang or dialect words and contractions and abbreviations. Connect your paragraphs with appropriate **discourse markers**.

When you're being polite you tend to use **modal verbs**, e.g. 'would', 'could', for example:
- I should be grateful if would let me have a copy.
- The children would be thrilled if they could go.

Discourse markers • Modal verb

Example Student Answer

This formal letter to an MP is written in an appropriate **register**.

9 Arthur Street
Rabbitsford
Yorkshire
RA5 7AZ
10/9/12

Ms Louisa Heaton MP
Kenilworth House
Dobbington

Dear Ms Heaton,

I am writing to express my concern about the lack of facilities available to young people in the Rabbitsford area.

I am a Year 11 student at the Kenilworth Academy and have lived in Rabbitsford all my life. The area has always lacked a great range of sports, leisure and social facilities but matters have been made a lot worse since the closure of the Gibbet Lane Youth Club earlier this year, where most young people in the area could meet and socialise.

As a result of this closure, under-18s now have nowhere to go after being dropped off by the school bus at 4.00pm.

The situation is made even worse by the lack of public transport. The last train back from Dobbington is 6.35pm and the buses are expensive and unreliable.

I am sure you will agree that the consequences of this could be serious for our community. As I am sure you are aware, vandalism and anti-social behaviour are already on the increase.

As Member of Parliament for Dobbington, you have always shown a keen interest in the problems facing young people in our area. I would ask you, therefore, to bring your influence to bear on the local council. A new youth centre and improved public transport for Rabbitsford would not cost a great deal of money and would have huge benefits for the community.

I look forward to hearing your views on my proposals.

Yours sincerely,
Michael Knightley

Commentary

- The letter is set out using proper letter conventions.
- An appropriate **formal register** is used.
- **Standard English** is used throughout.
- **Full words** are used instead of contractions, which add to the formal register.
- The writing has clear paragraph breaks.
- There is a clear opening paragraph.
- The correct sign off is used (to match the salutation).
- **Modal verbs** are used effectively to make suggestions and ensure the letter is polite.
- Effective **discourse markers** link the paragraphs and sentences well.

Quick Test

1. Read the four salutations below and decide on the correct way of signing off each letter:
   a) Dear Parents/Guardians
   b) Dear Dr Buckley
   c) Dear Ms Clover
   d) Dear Madam

Writing Leaflets

Audience and Purpose

A leaflet could be aimed at a **universal audience** or a specific **target audience**, depending on its content and purpose. If you're asked to write the text for a leaflet in your exam its purpose will probably be to inform, to explain, to persuade or to argue.

You'll be told the purpose and, if applicable, the intended audience. Look at the following examples – the first example has a specific target audience, while the second two do not.

Write the text for a leaflet aimed at GCSE students **explaining** how to deal with exams.

Write the text for a leaflet **persuading** people to support a charity of your choice.

Write the text for a leaflet in which you **argue** the case for more facilities for young people in your area.

Organisation and Presentation

You might have noticed that all the examples above ask you to **write the text** for a leaflet. They **do not** ask you to **design** a leaflet. The examiners do **not** want to see presentational devices such as columns, illustrations, charts, diagrams or different colours and fonts. You might not lose marks for including these devices, but you certainly will not gain any – and you'll have wasted time that should have been spent on writing the text.

You **should** include organisational devices such as:
- An effective **headline** – perhaps using a **pun** or **alliteration**. It doesn't have to be in huge letters and shouldn't be coloured in.

- **Subheadings** – to guide the reader through the text.
- **Paragraphs** – these tend to be short, but use them to show that you can.
- **Bullet points** – in most forms of writing these are not encouraged, but they are appropriate for leaflets. You might also use other organisational devices, such as numbering or arrows.
- **Text boxes** – these can help to show that you understand how leaflets are organised. But do not overuse them.

Language

The language you use will depend partly on your **audience** and **purpose**.

Leaflets are designed to make an impact quickly so they have a lot of simple sentences, short paragraphs and straightforward vocabulary.

When writing the text of a leaflet, make sure you:
- Attract the reader with techniques such as **puns, alliteration** and **rhyme**.

- Address your readers directly, perhaps using **questions** to involve them.
- Develop your ideas in detail.
- Use a variety of sentence structures.
- Use **varied vocabulary** that is appropriate for the content, purpose and audience.
- Use **modal verbs** and/or **imperatives** as appropriate.
- Use correct spelling and punctuation.

Key Words Headline • Subheading • Text box • Pun • Alliteration • Rhyme • Modal verb • Imperative

Example Student Answer

Here is part of an answer to this question:

Write the text for a leaflet aimed at GCSE students **explaining** how to deal with exams.

EXAMS – SHOW THEM WHO'S BOSS!

We've all got to do them. Some lucky so-and-sos have no problem with them – they're cool, they're calm and they're confident. Good for them! We'd all like to be like that but most of us find exams a bit more difficult and a lot more stressful. So what can we do to get the better of exam stress?

Get organised!

You're surrounded by teachers and parents banging on about revision – sometimes when you're only halfway through the course! If you're doing GCSEs you could be doing as many as ten subjects – and all the teachers think their subject is the most important and you should be spending half your waking hours revising it.

It's your future and you've got to take charge. Why not start by sitting down and making yourself a sensible, reasonable revision timetable that works for you? Think about:

- How many exams you'll be doing.
- When each exam takes place.
- Which subjects need the most work.
- How many hours' work per day you're comfortable doing.

Relax!

You know that saying about all work and no play making Jack a dull boy? Well, whether you're a boy or a girl, and whatever your name is, it's true. You need to relax. And you definitely need to include some down time in your plans...

Commentary

- This candidate is well-focused on purpose and audience – the purpose is to explain how to deal with exams. The writer has identified the main areas of concern for students and given them some advice on how to deal with them.
- The **tone** is friendly and quite **informal**, with contractions and informal punctuation, appropriate for a young audience.
- A few appropriate organisational devices are used – a **headline**, **subheadings** and **bullet points**.
- There is clear **paragraphing** and a good **variety of sentence structures**.
- The writer addresses the audience directly, using the **second person pronoun** 'you' as well as showing empathy by using the **first person plural pronoun** 'we'.
- A number of appropriate **linguistic devices** are used, e.g. **imperatives** in the headline and subheadings, **alliteration** and **rhetorical questions**, to appeal to the reader.

Think about how the language in this leaflet might differ if it had a different purpose (e.g. to persuade) and a different target audience.

Quick Test

1. Look again at the text above. Find an example of:
   a) An imperative,
   b) A minor sentence.
   c) Colloquial language.

Writing Newspaper Articles

Audience and Purpose

The audience for a newspaper article depends on the sort of newspaper it is printed in, e.g. a local paper, a tabloid or a broadsheet.

It's unlikely that a writing task in the exam would specify broadsheet or tabloid, but it might ask you to write for a local newspaper. It's possible that the article could be for a particular section of a newspaper with its own target audience, e.g. the women's page.

There are two main types of newspaper article: **reports** and **features**:

- **Reports** give the news. Their purpose is mainly to **inform** the reader but they might also **explain** some background.

- **Features** may be inspired by something in the news but they have a much wider range of purposes. They might **explain** what's happening in depth or they could be opinion pieces, which **argue** a case and/or try to **persuade** readers to a point of view. Some features seek mainly to entertain the reader. Others might focus on **describing** 'real life' stories.

In an exam you're more likely to be asked to write a feature than a report. You'll be told its purpose and, if applicable, the intended audience, for example:

> Write an article for your **local** newspaper in which you **describe** a life changing event.

> More and more teenagers are having cosmetic surgery. What are your views on this? Write an article for a newspaper's **women's** page giving your **arguments**.

The first task mentions a local newspaper. Your writing could make reference to local places and people and maybe use some local dialect.

For the second task, you'd probably focus on issues that affect women more than men and write in a friendly manner, looking for empathy from the readers, who might identify with the teenagers.

Organisation and Presentation

When writing a newspaper article, you are not expected to make your answer look like a newspaper. So you **should not** include:

- A masthead (title of the newspaper).
- Columns.
- Illustrations, charts and diagrams.

You **should** include organisational devices such as:

- A **headline**.
- A **strap line**.
- A **byline**, giving either your own name or a made up name.
- **Subheadings** or **cross heads**.
- **Paragraphs**.

In a newspaper **report** your first paragraph is very important. It should include:

- **Who**
- **What**
- **Where**
- **When**.

The second paragraph should expand on the first, giving a bit more detail.

The third and subsequent paragraphs should give more information and explanation, moving on to how and why.

Language

Newspaper articles, particularly those in tabloids, use simple vocabulary and sentences. But remember that in your exam you need to show you can write in a more sophisticated and mature way. Try to include common newspaper linguistic devices, such as:

* Alliteration
* Puns/play on words
* Emotive language.

Example Student Answer

Here is part of a student answer:

> COOL CAT MAKES A COMEBACK:
> A TALE OF TWO KITTIES
>
> 12-year-old moggy Arthur back from the dead.
> By Local Affairs Correspondent Olivia Fitch.
>
> Late last night local pet shop owner Grace Allbright got the shock of her life when Arthur the cat turned up fit and well on her doorstep in Miniver Avenue.
>
> Grace thought she had buried Arthur in the back garden of her suburban semi over three years ago.
>
> Arthur had been missing for two weeks in June 2009 when neighbour Keith Newton, 73, knocked on her door carrying the body of a black and white cat, wrapped in a towel. Peaceful and still. Grace still remembers it clearly. 'I was obviously devastated, but at the same time relieved to get some closure,' she recalled.
>
> Keith, who still lives two doors down, said he had found 'Arthur' in the gutter outside his house. Convinced of his identity, Keith had carefully wrapped Arthur in the towel and prepared to break the sad news to Grace.

Commentary

* The article has an effective headline which uses **alliteration** and **play on words**.
* The **strap line** expands on and explains the headline.
* A **byline** is included.
* The article is set in clear short paragraphs. (Paragraphs are usually quite short in local papers.)
* The first paragraph includes 'when, who, what and where'.
* **Present tense** is used in the headline to set the scene.
* **Past tense** is used for the rest of the report.
* Properly punctuated **direct speech** gives authenticity to the report.
* **Reported speech** is included, giving the name, age and description of the neighbour quoted.
* A variety of sentence types is used, including some short ones for effect.
* **Emotive language** is used to make the reader sympathise.

Quick Test

1 Look again at the article.
  a) Give details about 'who, what, where and when'.

  b) Give an example of a minor sentence or fragment.

Writing Magazine and Website Articles

Differences between Magazines and Newspapers

The main difference between magazines and newspapers is that magazines are less tied to news and current affairs. This affects the content of the articles but has no real effect on their **style**.

Writers of magazine and website articles may be more interested in **entertaining** their audience, so their articles are more likely to contain **humour**. The articles might also be longer and more thoughtful, with the writer expressing a personal opinion or writing about his/her own life, often using **anecdotes**. They're more likely to centre on stories where the focus is on an individual.

Audience and Purpose

Magazines and websites tend to be more **specialised** than newspapers.

If the exam question gives an audience, it could be:
* Men/Women
* Teenagers
* Younger children
* Older people
* Parents
* Teachers

School websites and school magazines often crop up. When writing for these you should remember that they're read by parents and teachers as well as by pupils.

There is a wide range of **purposes** you could be asked to write for and you could be asked to write either a report or a feature.

Examples of tasks you might be given are:

> Write a report for your school website **describing** a recent charity event held at the school.

> Write an article for a magazine aimed at teenagers **arguing** the case for or against the abolition of controlled assessment.

Both these articles could be written for a magazine or a website; there's no difference in the way you would write for a magazine or a website.

Organisation and Presentation

'Hard copy' magazines share many of the presentational features of newspapers. You'll see these on websites too but don't waste time trying to make your answer look like a magazine or website. You should include, however:
* A **headline**.
* A **strap line**.
* A **byline**.
* **Subheadings** or **cross heads**.
* **Paragraphs**.

If appropriate in the context of the task, a website article might also include **hyperlinks**, **text boxes** and **GUI widgets**.

Language

The language used in magazine and website articles is very similar to the language used in newspaper articles.

Try to include some effective **linguistic devices** when writing an article for a magazine or website.

Key Words   **Anecdote • Hyperlink • Linguistic device**

Example Student Answer

Here is part of an answer to this question. Think about how you'd continue this answer.

> Write an article for a **local news website** in which you **persuade** local people to support your campaign to save the Post Office.

Puddington Needs You!

And it certainly needs its Post Office, according to villager John Edwards

Alice Morris is eighty-three. She's lived in Little Billington all her life. I met her last week outside the Post Office in Puddington.

Alice was waiting for a taxi to take her the five miles back to her own village. It had dropped her off just half an hour before so she could collect her pension and buy a couple of bits and pieces. You see there's no post office in Little Billington. This is the nearest one for Alice and as she's got no car, there's no bus service and, in her own words she's 'a bit shaky on her pins', this is the only way for her to get around. It costs her fifteen pounds. A lot of money for a pensioner.

I've got bad news for Alice. If the Post Office has its way, she'll have to travel even further in future. You see, it's been announced that Puddington Post Office could close by the end of the year. Note that word 'could'. They've promised a consultation first.

I know what you're thinking: 'Consultation? They've made their minds up already!' Well, I'm as cynical as the next man. But do you know what? We can't afford cynicism. If they say they're going to consult us, we've got to make sure they do just that. If we don't want the Post Office to go the same way as the bus service, the village school, and the village bobby, we've got to stand up and be counted...

Commentary

- You can tell this is written for local people because the writer doesn't explain anything about Puddington. He also lets us know that he's local.
- The article has an effective exclamatory **headline** which uses the second person pronoun to instantly draw the reader in.
- A **strap line** and **byline** are included.
- The writer starts with an **anecdote**, an effective technique for an article like this.
- He uses the **first person** ('I' and 'we') showing that he's personally involved.
- He involves the readers by addressing them directly in the **second person** and asking **rhetorical questions**.
- He starts in the **past tense**, as he reports his meeting with Alice, but most of the article is written in the **present tense**.
- There is clear **paragraphing**, with the paragraphs varying in length, and a good **variety of sentence structures**.
- He uses a **conditional sentence** ('If...) to warn us about what will happen if we don't join his campaign.

Quick Test

1. How would you describe the register of the example above – formal or informal?
2. Why do you think the writer starts with his anecdote about Alice Morris?
3. Identify two 'lists of three' used for effect in the example above.

Writing Speeches

Why Write a Speech?

It is quite common for one of the exam tasks to involve writing the text for a speech.

You've probably given a speech as part of your Speaking and Listening controlled assessments.

For the exam, you are not actually going to give the speech so you must write out the entire speech as you'd like to give it. The trick is to make it *appear* natural and spontaneous!

Audience and Purpose

If you're asked to write a speech in your exam, it will be a speech that **you** would deliver. So the audience will be the kind of audience you might, in real life, be called upon to speak to, for example:

- Other students or teenagers your own age.
- Younger pupils.
- Your school assembly.
- Parents or governors.
- Teachers.

The content and style of your speech will differ according to your audience. If you're talking to people of your own age, the **tone** will probably be quite friendly and **colloquial**. But you'd probably be talking about a serious subject, so a certain **degree of formality** would be appropriate for all audiences.

Almost all tasks which ask you to write a speech will ask you to do one of two things:

- To **argue** a point of view **or**
- To **persuade** your audience to do something.

For example:

> Write a speech to be presented to your class in which you **argue** for the right to vote at 16.

> Write a speech to be given at a school assembly **persuading** fellow students to vote for you as Head Girl or Boy.

Organisation and Presentation

When writing a speech, you don't need to use any specific presentational devices and it should follow the conventions for any essay. Write in **full sentences** and in **paragraphs**. Don't use abbreviations, bullet points or illustrations.

It's important that you:

- Start with a **strong opening paragraph**, which grabs the audience's attention and introduces your topic.
- Build your argument logically, using **discourse markers** to guide your audience.
- End with a **strong concluding paragraph**, which briefly sums up your points and leaves the audience with something to think about.

Rhetoric: The Language of Speeches

Rhetoric means the art of speaking. **Rhetorical devices** are the 'tricks' that good speakers use to put their case to an audience. If you're writing a speech, it's essential that you include some of them.

Personal Pronouns

- You must engage your audience so you'll use the **second person** plural pronoun ('you') a lot. Because 'you' is also singular, there are times when an individual member of the audience might feel personally addressed by 'you'.
- You'll use the **first person** ('I', 'we') more often than in most forms of writing. This shows that you identify and empathise with your audience.
- You might occasionally want to use a different form of address e.g. 'fellow students' or 'friends'.

Structural Devices

- **Rhetorical questions** are questions which don't expect an answer. Sometimes speakers answer rhetorical questions themselves, e.g. 'Are we going to win this election? You bet we are!'. But it can be more effective to leave listeners to answer it, e.g. 'Do we really want our children growing up in a country like that?'
- **The rule of three** could be three points in a row, three questions or three examples, e.g. 'Restructuring the system would be an expensive, time-consuming and unworkable nightmare'.
- **Lists** can emphasise the extent of something, e.g. listing all the countries that have banned whale hunting.

- **Repetition** emphasises key points so that they stick in the audience's mind.
- **Parallel phrasing** means repeating the structure and some of the vocabulary of phrases or sentences, e.g. 'I have a dream that one day this nation… I have a dream that one day on the red hills'.
- **Imperatives** are commands, which can be very effective: 'Go out and change the world!'

Diction

- **Emotive language** is used to manipulate the audience's feelings, e.g. 'This lonely, desperate child urgently needs your help'.
- **Superlatives** are used to express extremes, e.g. 'Last year was the best year ever for sales'.
- **Alliteration** can reflect the speaker's emotions, e.g. harsh 'k' sounds can convey anger.
- **Figurative language**, such as **similes** and **metaphors** can be very effective.

Argument and Counter Argument

Although speeches often express very strong views, it's a good idea to give both sides of an argument before arguing against one. For example:

> There are some who claim that a smoking ban infringes their civil rights. I say, what about our rights? Our right not to breathe in foul air; our right not to have smoke blown in our faces; our right not to contract diseases from your filthy habit?

Quick Test

1. Of which rhetorical device are the following examples?
   a) We shall fight on the beaches, we shall fight on the landing grounds…
   b) What kind of people do they think we are?
   c) Ask not what your country can do for you…
   d) Youth is a blunder; manhood a struggle; old age a regret.

Writing Discursive Essays

What is a Discursive Essay?

A **discursive essay** is a piece of writing in which you discuss a topic.

If you get a question in the exam that requires you to write a discursive essay, you may or may not be specifically asked to 'write an essay', for example:

> You have been invited to enter a writing competition. Your task is to write an essay **arguing** the case for or against fox hunting. Write your entry.

> 'In today's society beauty is valued above brains'. Do you agree or disagree with this proposition? **Argue** your case.

> **Describe** how you think life will be in thirty years' time.

If the question doesn't specify the form (e.g. letter, article) you'll be writing an essay. This sort of question is more likely at Higher Tier than Foundation Tier.

Audience and Purpose

When writing a discursive essay you don't need to write as if you're addressing a different audience. You don't know who'll be examining your work but you can assume it will be an intelligent adult, so you should write in a mature, formal style.

The purpose of your essay could be to argue, describe, inform, explain or persuade.

Organisation and Presentation

When writing an essay, you should:
- Write in clear **paragraphs**.
- Start with a **strong opening paragraph**, which introduces your topic concisely and effectively. Good essays often start by 'questioning the question' – trying to define what it means.
- Use **discourse markers** to guide your audience.

- **Build your argument** logically through the following paragraphs (ensuring that you consider the other side of the argument if you're writing to argue).
- End with a **strong concluding paragraph**, which sums up your points and makes your opinion clear but leaves the audience with plenty to think about.

Language

Essays tend to be more thoughtful and reflective in **tone** than other forms of writing and the language you use should reflect this.

You should use a **formal register**. Many of the **rhetorical devices** described on page 73 can be very effective in essays.

To help give the essay a more serious tone you should try to use:
- The **passive voice**.
- Varied sentence structures.
- **Modal verbs**.
- Varied, and ambitious **vocabulary**.
- **Evidence**, e.g. statistics (you might find these in the sources for your reading questions).

Key Words   **Paragraph • Discourse marker • Passive voice • Modal verb • Evidence**

Language (cont.)

You can also add a personal touch by using the **first person**, and adding an **anecdote** or **humour**.

Avoid using **direct address**, **contractions**, **imperatives**, **slang** and non-Standard English.

Example Answer

Here is part of an answer to this question:

> 'In today's society, beauty is valued above brains'. Do you agree or disagree with this proposition? **Argue** your case.

It surrounds and attacks us every day of our lives. The media seem to be obsessed by it. Newspapers, magazines and television tell us how we should look, undermining our confidence with their never-ending parade of perfect bodies and desirable faces. But do these images represent beauty? And, even if they do, is it truly being valued above brains by our society?

I would argue that society as a whole does not value beauty above brains. First, we must ask how we know what 'society' thinks or feels as a whole. We could use the media as a yardstick, certainly, and on that basis might well agree with the statement. Much of the media is devoted to the superficial. Pages and pages are dedicated not only to articles about those deemed to be beautiful, but also to advice columns on how to attract the opposite sex, features on how to look your best, and adverts for fashion and beauty products. Beauty and the pursuit of beauty sell. Therefore, a huge number of people must value it very highly.

However, the fact that many people value beauty does not mean that they necessarily value it more than brains. Can they not value both?

Commentary

- The answer engages the readers' interest with a short, strong opening statement.
- It is clearly paragraphed: the first paragraph picks up on the statement and questions it; the second paragraph states the writer's point of view but goes on to give the other side of the argument; the third paragraph starts a counter argument. We would expect the writer to develop the point made in this paragraph, and argue that the media's apparent obsession with beauty does not prove that society values it above brains.
- **Discourse markers** are used effectively.
- A variety of sentence structures is used.
- The **vocabulary** is varied and ambitious.
- Rhetorical devices are used – rhetorical questions, parallel phrasing, alliteration and emotive and figurative language.
- The **passive voice** is used.

Quick Test

1 In the essay above, look at the second paragraph and find:
   a) Use of the passive voice. **b)** A modal verb. **c)** A list of three.

Writing to Inform

Information

The **first** (shorter) task in the writing section of your exam will ask you to write to inform, explain or describe.

When you **inform** people about something, you're simply telling them what you know. After reading a piece of informative writing, readers should feel that they've learned something they didn't know before.

It's likely that you might be asked to **inform and describe** or to **inform and explain**. Even if you were only asked to 'inform', a full answer would involve a certain amount of description and explanation.

Content

Information texts can cover a wide variety of subjects. Things you could be asked to inform someone about include:

*   An aspect of life in school.
*   Your local area.
*   A hobby, sport or leisure interest.
*   Your family or friends.

The question will let you choose something you know about. For example, you could be asked to write a leaflet about 'a sport or hobby' as everyone can then think of something to write about.

You could be asked to inform about something that's already happened, that's happening now or that will happen in the future.

Form

Information can be conveyed in any form, for example:

*   An informal **letter** informing a friend or relative of your plans for the future.
*   A **leaflet** giving information about tourist attractions in your area.
*   An **article** for a newspaper, magazine or website giving information about your school.
*   The text for a **speech** in which you inform about the life of someone you admire.

Things to Consider When Writing to Inform

When writing to inform you should:

*   Start with a strong, **clear opening paragraph**, to tell your readers what the text will be about.
*   Include all relevant aspects of your subject.
*   Make your points in a **logical order** (a quick plan will help you decide on the right order), using **discourse markers** to add further information.
*   Sum up your points effectively in a final paragraph and leave the readers feeling that they've learned something.

*   Include **facts**, perhaps even **statistics** – the examiner will not mind if you make them up.
*   Use **specialised** or **technical language** if appropriate, but explain it as you're writing for people who don't know the subject.
*   Think about whether a formal or informal **tone** is most appropriate. For a general audience, a formal tone is better.
*   Use **subheadings** and **bullet points**, if appropriate, to break up the text.

Key Words   **Discourse marker • Fact • Statistics • Subheading**

Example of Writing to Inform

Here is an answer to a 'writing to inform' task:

> Write a letter to your head teacher informing him or her about the environment of your school or college and the effect it has on the students.

14 Alder Avenue
Worthington

Mr J R Fletcher
Principal
Greenacres Technology College

12 April 2012

Dear Mr Fletcher,

I am writing, on behalf of the student council of Greenacres College, to inform you of our concerns about the environment. When I use the word 'environment', I refer not to the state of the planet, the plight of the world's wildlife or the future of the eco-system, but to the everyday environment in which we all work.

We students have become very concerned lately about the amount of litter to be found around the school. Almost every day, students arrive in their classrooms to find the floors are covered in all manner of detritus: sweet wrappers, empty crisp packets, and discarded drink cans. Desks are embellished daily with fresh graffiti and their undersides studded with stale gum.

The corridors are even worse. Very few bins are provided and they are all overflowing with litter. Small, plastic, swing-top bins, designed for suburban kitchens, are clearly not adequate for the needs of a busy college like ours. Again, there is graffiti, with notice boards continually defaced. Can you imagine how it feels to see your beautifully presented, proudly displayed work violated by the crudest of obscenities?

Finally, I turn to the foyer – the first and last impression received by any visitor. Not the warmest of welcomes. It is drab. It is uncared for. It is unfriendly. No stranger who enters that space could fail to be underwhelmed; no distinguished visitor could leave it without a sense of relief.

These are the facts which I place before you on behalf of my fellow students. I should be most grateful if you, as Principal of Greenacres College, would give them the consideration they deserve. We, the students, would be happy to present you with our own proposals for improvement. I look forward to receiving your response.

Yours sincerely

Samira Miah

Commentary

- Although the task is to **inform** the Principal about the environment, the writer needs to give some explanation in order to develop her points.
- The writer is presenting facts but, in this case, the letter is not entirely unbiased. She would not be describing these things if she felt they were acceptable.
- The opening paragraph tells us what the letter will be about and each subsequent paragraph tells us about a new aspect of the problem, with the final paragraph summing up and inviting a reply.
- Discourse markers are used effectively to build up a case by adding information.
- The language is fairly **formal**, with modal verbs, full words rather than **contractions** and the **passive voice** contributing to its polite tone.
- There are **rhetorical devices** such as rhetorical questions, the 'rule of three' and parallel phrasing.
- A full range of **sentence structures** and a varied **vocabulary** are used.

Quick Test

1. Look again at the letter above.
   a) What tense is most of the letter written in?
   b) Is this a formal or an informal letter?
   c) What is the topic of each of the second, third and fourth paragraphs?
   d) What do you think the writer wants from the recipient?

Writing to Explain

Explanation

In the **first** task in the writing section of the exam, you may be asked to **explain**.

Explanation means going into more detail and writing about 'how' and 'why' as well as 'who', 'what', 'where' and 'when'.

After reading a text whose purpose is to explain, readers should clearly understand a subject.

Content

Just as with 'inform' questions, you will not be asked to write about a particular subject. The task will be quite general.

Often you'll be asked to **inform and explain** or to **describe and explain**. You might be asked to explain 'why' or 'how'.

For example:
* Why you enjoy something you do.
* Why you like or admire someone or something.
* How to do something.
* How something works.

Form

You could be asked to write in any form, for example:
* A **letter** to a local paper informing people about a voluntary group and explaining what it does.
* A **leaflet** explaining how to organise revision.

* An **article** for a website describing a personal experience and explaining its effect on you.
* The text for a **speech** in which you inform your audience about the life of someone you admire and explain why you admire him or her.

Things to Consider When Writing to Explain

When writing to explain you should:
* Start with a strong opening paragraph, in which you introduce the topic and 'hook' your readers.
* Make sure that every paragraph includes some explanation – always be looking at 'how' or 'why'.
* Use **discourse markers** to develop your points and give order to your writing.
* Make sure that the final paragraph effectively sums up the 'why' or 'how'.
* Give appropriate examples, perhaps using **anecdotes**.
* Think about whether a formal or informal **tone** is most appropriate.

* Use **specialised** or **technical language** if appropriate, but explain it as you're not writing for people who know the subject.
* Think about whether to write in the **past** or **present tense**: if you're explaining how to do something, use the present tense; if you're explaining why or how you did something, use the past tense.
* If you're explaining 'how to', use the **second person** ('you'), **modal verbs** such as 'you should', and **imperatives**.
* Use **subheadings** and **bullet points**, if appropriate, to break up the text.

Key Words Discourse marker • Past tense • Present tense • Second person • Modal verb • Imperative

Example of Writing to Explain

Here is an answer to a 'writing to explain' task:

> Write an article for a website, aimed at Year 10 pupils, **explaining** how to approach work experience. Remember to:
> - Write an article.
> - Write for Year 10 pupils.
> - Write to explain.

WORK: EXPERIENCE OF A LIFETIME OR EXPERIENCE TO FORGET?

Our guide to surviving work experience

Some of us look forward to it; others dread it. Most of us probably have mixed feelings. And it's no wonder. In a few months' time your routine will be changed, and your life turned upside-down. You'll be snatched from the warm comforting security blanket of school. And plunged... into what? If all goes well, it could be the experience of your life. Whether it is or not depends on how you approach it. So here are some ideas on how to make the most of work experience.

Finding the right job

First things first. Get yourself the right job. You'll probably be given the option of finding your own placement, which means asking family and friends of family if they know of anything suitable. So how do you find the job that's right for you? Here are a few things to think about:
- Does it sound enjoyable?
- Is it something you'd consider doing when you leave school?
- Has the employer got a good reputation?

The more you know, the better placed you are to make a good choice.

First impressions

First impressions really do matter. So be sure to make the right impression on your employers from the start.

First and foremost, be punctual! To make sure you're not going to be late, study bus or train timetables beforehand. Better to be half an hour early than five minutes late.

You should also make sure that you dress appropriately. In some jobs a uniform is provided. Others, however, just tell you to be 'smart', while others say they have no dress code. Whatever they say, it's better to be too smart than not smart enough. Aim to look neat and tidy.

And of course, be polite. Good manners are important in all walks of life. Some work places are more formal than others. It's a good idea to take your lead from the person assigned to look after you.

Commentary

- The task is to explain how to approach work experience. So the candidate gives a series of fairly detailed suggestions.
- The answer explains **how** pupils could find a placement and how they should act, as well as **why** things like being punctual matter.
- The writer addresses the readers directly ('you') and shows empathy with them by using the first person plural pronoun ('us').
- A lot of imperatives are used, as well as modal verbs.
- Rhetorical questions are used to make the readers think.
- There is a **friendly tone**, appropriate to Year 10 but **Standard English** is used.
- The opening paragraph tells us what the article is for. Each subsequent paragraph looks at a new aspect of work experience. The rest of the answer might look at fitting in with colleagues and what might be learned from the experience.
- The article is written in paragraphs but is also broken up effectively by subheadings.
- Although the paragraphs are fairly short and there are quite a lot of short sentences, there is still a good range of sentence structures.

Quick Test

1. Look at the first paragraph of the answer above and find:
   a) A metaphor.
   b) An example of ellipsis.
   c) A conditional sentence.

Writing to Describe

Description

In the **first** task of the writing section of the exam, you may be asked to **describe**.

Descriptive writing gives information to readers, and often explains too, but it can give scope for using language more creatively and developing a personal viewpoint.

You'll be familiar with descriptive writing from the creative writing controlled assessment. But in this exam you'll be asked to describe something real, rather than imagined.

Content

Don't feel that you have to describe something exotic or unusual. It's the quality of your writing that makes the description interesting, not its subject matter.

This exam is about non-fiction writing so the tasks will ask you to write about something you know or have experienced such as a place, a person or a personal experience.

Form

You could be asked to write in any form, but the most likely are letters and articles. For example:
- A **letter** to a pen-friend describing your neighbourhood.
- An **article** for a website describing a journey.
- A **letter** to a newspaper describing someone who you feel has made a contribution to the community.
- An **article** for a magazine describing a life changing experience.

Things to Consider When Writing to Describe

When writing to describe you should:
- Start with a paragraph that **intrigues** and 'draws in' the reader.
- Think about different aspects of your subject that you could describe – they don't all have to be positive!
- Consider all **five senses** – sight, hearing, smell, taste and touch.
- Maybe use the **'big-to-small' technique**, starting with what something is like from a distance and then moving in closer.
- If you're writing a description of something that's happened to you, you'll need to use the **first person**. In other types of description you may or may not want to include personal feelings.
- Use **figurative language**, including **metaphors** and **similes**.
- Think about whether to write in the **past** or **present tense**: both can be effective.
- Use **adjectives** and **adverbs**.
- Use literary techniques such as **alliteration** (e.g. 'clasped in crooked claws'), **assonance** (e.g. 'gloomy blue rooms') and **onomatopoeia** (e.g. 'the fizz of fireworks').
- Use discourse markers to help move the writing along.
- Use both **active** and **passive voices**.
- Vary your sentence lengths and use techniques such as **parallel phrasing** and **fragments**.
- Be adventurous with your choice of vocabulary.
- You are **not** writing a story, but you could still write a **chronological** account of an experience.

Key Words   Metaphor • Simile • Alliteration • Assonance • Onomatopoeia • Parallel phrasing

Example of Writing to Describe

Here is an answer to a 'writing to describe' task:

> Write an article for a magazine describing a place you have visited recently.

It is cold. Yet the sun blazes golden, cradled in a hard blue sky. Silence. To the right a neat, rounded, still verdant mound thrusts confidently towards it. Its regularity suggests something shaped by man. But which men? Who were these ancient people who laboured, without machinery, to create something as pleasing to the mathematician's eye as to the artist's, something as grand and as beautiful as the great cathedral domes of London, Florence and Rome? Perhaps it was carved from the hill to worship their gods and bear witness to their power, or perhaps its purpose was more sinister: an act of aggression or of desperation, built to defend the last remnants of their civilisation.

Strangely, the snow has not touched this hill. Its neighbour, to our left, has not been spared. The irregular contours of the sleeping giant are draped in a soft cloak of virgin white. Its soft outlines invite us. We do not resist. As we start our climb, the only sound is of boots breaking the crisp morning snowfall. If we stop, the silence is unbroken. The wind stings and caresses in turn. A solitary kestrel swoops, smoothly cutting the air, following a prey seen only by itself.

Suddenly there are voices and we realise we are not alone. Just above us we can see and hear, on their way down, a young couple. On their way down! It is barely eight o'clock in the morning. What time did they start their climb? They are still full of vigour, laughing as they chase each other, tripping in the snow and helping each other up, stopping for a brief embrace.

The serenity of the hills is broken, but only for a moment. They pass and others do too. Still others follow us to the top to rest for a moment in exhausted triumph. There we are all stilled by the majesty of the winter landscape. The hills that watched when those ancient people built their temple or fort are watching us now, and they will watch long after we have gone.

Commentary

- The description starts without explanation. We don't know where we are or why but we are drawn in straightaway.
- Although it isn't a story, the account is in **chronological order**.
- It is written mainly in the **present tense**, as if the writer is experiencing it now, which makes the descriptions more vivid.
- It is written in the **first person**, but the narrator does not 'intrude' – the landscape is more important.
- Adjectives and adverbs are used effectively.
- **Imagery** is used, including metaphor, simile and personification to make the scene 'come alive'.
- **Alliteration** is used to emphasise certain descriptions.
- Both **active** and **passive** voices are used.
- The writing contains **rhetorical questions**, **repetition** and the **'rule of three'**.
- There is a variety of sentence structures and a varied, **ambitious vocabulary**.

Quick Test

1. Look again at the answer above. In the first paragraph find an example of:
   a) A minor sentence or fragment.
   b) Alliteration.
   c) Repetition.

Writing to Argue

Argument

For the **second** writing task in your exam you'll be asked to argue or persuade. You're expected to spend longer on this task than on the first task (about 35 minutes).

Writing to argue means expressing a point of view as clearly and effectively as you can. There are (at least) two sides to every argument. You may be told which side to argue for, but you're more likely to be given the choice of arguing for or against something, allowing you to express your real point of view.

Content

It's likely that a writing to argue task will be based on something that most people of your age would have an opinion about. This could mean issues that are often discussed in school and in the media, such as fox hunting, global warming or cosmetic surgery. But it's more likely to be something closer to home that affects everyone of your age, such as homework or local facilities for young people.

Form

You could be asked to write in any form, for example:

- A **letter** to a local councillor arguing that more should be done to improve leisure facilities for young people.
- A **leaflet** arguing that you should be elected as Head Girl or Head Boy.
- An **article** for a website arguing against experiments on animals.
- The text for a **speech** to be given to your school governors in which you argue that homework should be abolished.
- An **essay** entitled 'Work Experience: Taste of Real Life or Waste of Two Weeks?'.

Things to Consider when Writing to Argue

When writing to argue you should:

- Start with a **powerful opening paragraph**, which grabs your audience's attention and makes your point clear.
- Offer a number of points in support of your argument and start a new paragraph for each.
- Acknowledge **other points of view** but then give your **counter arguments**, pointing out why you think they're wrong.
- Structure your argument in a logical order.
- Use **discourse markers** to 'signpost' the logical development of your argument.
- Back up your points with evidence if possible.
- Give appropriate examples, including **anecdotes**.
- Think about whether a formal or informal tone is most appropriate.
- Address your audience directly, using 'you' and show your own involvement by using 'I' and 'we'.
- Use a full range of **rhetorical devices**.
- Use **hyperbole**, exaggerating your points to capture the audience's attention.
- Add **humour** if you think it's appropriate.
- Use a variety of sentence structures.
- Finish with a **strong conclusion**, in which you sum up the main points and state your opinion.

Counter argument • Discourse marker • Anecdote • Hyperbole

Example of Writing to Argue

Here is an answer to a 'writing to argue' task:

> Write an essay entitled 'Work Experience: Taste of Real Life or Waste of Two Weeks?'

Work Experience: Taste of Real Life or Waste of Two Weeks?

Work experience is an established and accepted part of today's school calendar. But why? There are still people around – your grandparents perhaps or some elderly teachers – who can remember a time before work experience and might just remember whose idea it was originally and why people thought it was a good idea at the time. For the rest of us it's a mystery.

I decided to ask around and found the general opinion amongst the adults I asked was that it would prepare young people for the world of work. I have to say, though, that none of them (not even the careers teacher) sounded terribly convinced. One harassed teacher, admittedly, did say it was 'to get you lot out of our hair for a few days!'. Honest, yes, but probably not what the government that established work experience had in mind.

So, assuming the object of the exercise is to prepare us for the world of work, does it? And, more fundamentally, do we need it to? First, I would like to consider how, if at all, two weeks of work experience prepares us for work. My placement was in my uncle's office. He is a solicitor and the rationale behind the placement was that I had expressed an interest in studying Law. But what did I learn? I learned that you should dress smartly and be punctual. I learned how to answer the telephone politely. I learned that solicitors drink an awful lot of coffee. I could have found out all of that just by having a chat with my uncle.

Nevertheless, many people would argue it was useful to find out what it's really like to get up every morning, get dressed smartly and make sure I arrive at my destination on time and ready to do whatever I might be told to do. But I already do that. It's called school.

Commentary

- The opening paragraph establishes the **tone** and makes it clear which side of the argument the writer is on.
- **Discourse markers** are used to 'signpost' the argument.
- **Hyperbole** is used to overstate the case in the first paragraph.
- The first person ('I' 'we', 'us') is used to show the writer's strong personal interest in the subject.
- **Rhetorical questions** are used to involve the audience.
- A personal **anecdote** is used to illustrate the writer's point.
- Acknowledges the other side of the argument before using humour to dismiss it.
- The writer includes evidence to back up his argument.
- The language is mostly formal but there are informal touches, such as using **contractions**.
- There is a humorous, even **sarcastic**, **tone** to the essay.
- There is a good variety of sentence structures.

Quick Test

1. Does the writer think work experience is worthwhile?
2. According to the second paragraph, does the writer think that there is any real support for work experience?
3. What tense does the writer use for the personal anecdote in paragraph three?

Writing to Persuade

Persuasion

For the **second** writing task in your exam you may be asked to persuade.

Writing to persuade and writing to argue are similar in many ways. When you argue a point of view you're usually trying to persuade your audience that you're right. But writing to persuade someone to do something, feel something or think a certain way involves other ways of influencing them.

You have to consider not only what you want to achieve but also what might stop people wanting to do what you want them to do.

Content

In our everyday lives we're surrounded by persuasive writing. In your exam you might be asked to promote an invented product. But it's more likely that you'd be asked to persuade someone to do something for charity or the community.

Form

You could be asked to write in any form, for example:
- An informal **letter** to a friend persuading him or her to come on holiday with you.
- A **letter** to an MP to persuade him/her to stop a new supermarket opening in your area.
- A **leaflet** persuading people to join your local youth centre or club.
- An **article** for a website or magazine advertising a new product or service.
- The text for a **speech** to be given to your year group's assembly in which you persuade your audience to become mentors for younger pupils.

Things to Consider When Writing to Persuade

When writing to persuade you should:
- Start with a **powerful opening**, which grabs your audience's attention.
- Make a variety of points, logically structured in paragraphs.
- Use **discourse markers** to connect points.
- Flatter your readers, e.g. 'I have always admired the way you stand up for your beliefs…'.
- Involve your readers by addressing them using 'you' and by identifying with them using 'we'.
- Be polite, using **modal verbs**.
- Use **conditional sentences**, making suggestions about what might happen.
- Back up your points with **evidence** if possible.
- Give appropriate examples, including **anecdotes**.
- Think about whether a formal or informal **tone** is most appropriate.
- Use a full range of **rhetorical devices**.
- Use **hyperbole**, exaggerating your points to capture the audience's attention.
- Use **emotive language** to influence your readers.
- Use a variety of sentence structures.
- Finish with a **strong conclusion**, in which you sum up the main points and make a strong appeal to your readers.

Key Words   Discourse marker • Modal verb • Conditional sentence • Anecdote • Hyperbole

Example of Writing to Persuade

Here is an answer to a 'writing to persuade' task:

> Write a letter to an MP to persuade him/her to stop a new supermarket opening in your area.

22 Keble Street
Toddington
Lancashire

Alicia Pirelli MP
House of Commons
London

14th July 2012

Dear Ms Pirelli,

I am writing to express my opposition to the proposed supermarket on St. Andrew's playing field in Toddington. I am especially concerned that the local council appears to support the proposal. However I know that you, since being elected as our MP last year, have campaigned tirelessly for the preservation of green spaces in our towns. We, the residents of the area around St. Andrew's, share your concerns and are appealing to you to help us save our field.

I realise that, since St. Andrew's High School was pulled down, the field has not been used for its original purpose. I also understand that the council is short of money and will see the sale of the land as a good opportunity to raise some much needed money.

Nevertheless, I believe that this is a short-sighted idea and that once the field is gone, we will regret a lost opportunity. Children will have nowhere to play except in the busy streets. It is criminal that they are put in danger every day when they could be playing safely on the field. And what about their health? Rising obesity levels amongst children are constantly in the news. To combat this we need space to exercise in, not outlets for fast food, pop and sweets.

I know that many people say we need a new supermarket in Toddington. I understand, too, that the proposed development might bring much-needed jobs to the area, but I am afraid that this development could have the opposite effect. There are many small, traditional shops and businesses in this part of town and they would undoubtedly suffer, possibly leading to the loss of more jobs than the supermarket would create.

In addition, congestion would be a major problem with this site.

If Toddington really does need a supermarket, there must be somewhere better to put it. Let's not sacrifice what little green we have left in Toddington. I should be most grateful if you would give us your support in trying to save St Andrew's field.

Yours sincerely
Barry Wong

Commentary

- The opening statement grabs the reader's attention and states the purpose.
- Several different points are made in support of the writer's point of view.
- **Connectives/discourse markers** used.
- The first person ('I' 'we', 'our') is used to show the writer's personal interest in the subject.
- The writer flatters the reader to get her 'on side'.
- The writer acknowledges the opposite point of view and deals with it by **counter argument**.
- **Rhetorical devices** such as rhetorical questions and lists of three are used.
- **Emotive language** and **hyperbole** play on the reader's feelings.
- The tone is formal and polite, with **modal verbs** and **conditionals**.
- The final paragraph tells the reader what the writer wants her to do.

Quick Test

1. **a)** How does the writer show that there is support for his view?
   b) Which connectives does he use to introduce contrasting ideas?
   c) Which connectives does he use to introduce additional points?

Key Words | Emotive language | 85

Section B of the Foundation Tier exam will consist of two questions: 6 and 7. Here are three examples of each question.

- *You will need to answer both questions.*
- *You are advised to spend about 25 minutes on question 6 and about 35 minutes on question 7.*

6. Write a **letter** to a friend who lives in another country **describing** a hobby or pastime that you enjoy and **explaining** why you enjoy it.

   Remember to:
   - write about a hobby
   - write a letter
   - write to describe and explain. *(16 marks)*

7. Write the text for a **speech** you have been asked to give to your year group, **arguing** that school uniforms are **either** a good thing or a bad thing.

   Remember to:
   - write a speech
   - argue either for or against school uniforms. *(24 marks)*

6. Write an **article** for a teenage magazine about a favourite film or TV programme and **explain** why you like it.

   Remember to:
   - write about a film or TV programme
   - write an article for teenagers
   - write to explain. *(16 marks)*

7. Write the text for a **leaflet** in which you try to **persuade** people to support a charity of your choice.

   Remember to:
   - write the text for a leaflet
   - write about a charity
   - write to persuade. *(24 marks)*

6. Write the text for a **leaflet**, aimed at new pupils at your school, **informing** them about activities that are on offer at the school and **explaining** how they can get involved.

   Remember to:
   - write about activities at your school
   - write the text for a leaflet
   - write to inform and explain. *(16 marks)*

7. You would like a holiday job at a local shop or business, which you know well. Write a **letter** to the manager, **persuading** him or her to let you work there.

   Remember to:
   - write a letter
   - write to **persuade.** *(24 marks)*

Section B of the Higher Tier exam will consist of two questions: 5 and 6. Here are four examples of each question.

- *You will need to answer both questions.*
- *You are advised to spend about 25 minutes on question 5 and about 35 minutes on question 6.*

---

5. Write an article for a teenage magazine describing an important event in your life and explaining its effect on you. *(16 marks)*

6. Write the text for a speech you have been invited to give to your school's governors, arguing that school uniforms are **either** a good thing or a bad thing. *(24 marks)*

---

5. Write the text for a leaflet informing visitors about attractions in your local area. *(16 marks)*

6. Write a letter to your local MP or councillor arguing that young people should be allowed to vote in elections from the age of 16. *(24 marks)*

---

5. You have recently returned from a school trip. Write an article for your school website describing the trip. *(16 marks)*

6. Write a letter to your local newspaper to try to persuade local people to take more care of their environment. *(24 marks)*

---

5. Write a letter to an older relative informing him or her of what you plan to do after you leave school and explaining your choices. *(16 marks)*

6. 'Young people today spend too much time thinking about themselves and not enough thinking of others'. Argue the case **for or against** this idea. *(24 marks)*

Quick Test Answers

Page 7
1. To persuade.
2. Girls aged approximately 16–25.
3. To explain and instruct.
4. New mothers (and fathers).

Page 9
1. A true statement.
2. Someone's point of view.
3. Opinion.
4. To convince the reader that it is a fact.

Page 11
1. Working out a meaning that isn't obvious.
2. The reader.
3. Feelings, Attitude, Intentions, Opinion.
4. Inference.

Page 13
1. Language used in a particular region.
2. Adverb.
3. To arouse feelings in the readers.
4. Exaggeration.

Page 15
1. To list information.
2. A newspaper report.
3. **Any from:** Colour, Bold, Italic, Underline, Font style, Font size.
4. They can make information easier to understand.

Page 17
1. It was traditionally bigger than a tabloid.
2. To inform and explain.
3. Local.
4. Explains the headline.

Page 19
1. A teenage magazine.
2. People interested in baking.
3. Someone in a relationship with a woman.

Page 21
1. You.
2. A catchphrase associated with a company or product.
3. A charity advert.

Page 23
1. **a)** 'Dirty, dishevelled and degraded'; 'zap those zits!'
   b) **Any two from:** Clean; Take; Follow; Zap.
   c) Me.
   d) **Any from:** You; Your.

Page 25
1. **a)** First person.
   b) To highlight a section where you can find extra information.

Page 27
1. **a)** His memory is hazy.
   b) To make the scene more vivid.
   c) He wouldn't remember the name.
   d) 'Noiselessly'. It's effective because it describes how the dog managed to take the meat with no one noticing.

Page 29
1. **a)** Extract from a Guide Book.
   b) *Pictures from Italy.*
   c) *Pictures from Italy.*
   d) Extract from a Guide Book.

Page 31
1. **a)** 'like a hungry wolf'
   b) **Any from:** 'a triumph', 'not to be missed', 'truly menacing', 'almost faultless'.

Page 33
1. **a)** **Any two from:** 'Saving the lives', 'We never destroy a healthy dog'; 'give a happy home'; 'Stray and abandoned dogs'; 'little lives so much happier!'
   b) **Any three from:** Donate money; Become a member of the Trust; Support your local rehoming centre; Take part in sporting challenges; Get involved in fundraising.
   c) They show healthy, happy dogs that could inspire readers to want to help other dogs.

Page 35
1. **a)** Text B.
   b) Both.
   c) Both.

Page 37
1. **a)** Text B.
   b) Text A.
   c) Text A.

Page 49
1. **a)** The dog had disappeared. There was no doubt about that. (Alternatively, you might use a semi-colon after 'disappeared' and a lower case 't' in 'there'.)
   b) 'Where's my dog?' she cried. 'Bring him back!'
   c) The dog's owner was not happy, however, when it jumped on the stage.
   d) The magician, who was remarkably tall and fat, acknowledged the audience's applause. (Alternatively, you might use brackets around 'who was remarkably tall and fat'.)

Page 51

1. **a)** Compound sentence.
   b) Minor sentence (fragment).
   c) Simple sentence.
   d) Complex sentence.

Page 53

1. **a)** practise.   **c)** It's.
   b) where… were.   **d)** whether.

Page 55

1. **a)** Jay and I were put on detention.
   b) I saw you on Saturday.
   c) You were the best player we had.
   d) We'd sung the first one so afterwards we did a dance.

Page 57

1. By indenting.
2. **Any two from**: Change of speaker, person, place, time, topic/idea.

Page 59

1. **a)** 'Basically' – to sum up.
   b) 'On the other hand' – to express difference or contrast.
   c) 'Before' – to denote time.
   d) 'Therefore' – to express cause and effect.

Page 61

1. **a)** Informal.   **c)** Formal.
   b) Formal.   **d)** Informal.

Page 63

1. **a)** Formal.   **c)** Informal.
   b) Informal.   **d)** Formal.

Page 65

1. **a)** Yours faithfully.   **c)** Yours sincerely.
   b) Yours sincerely.   **d)** Yours faithfully.

Page 67

1. **a)** **Any from:** 'Show them who's boss!', 'Get organised!', 'Think about', 'Relax!'.
   b) 'Good for them!'
   c) **Any from**: 'So-and-sos', 'cool', 'banging on', 'down time'.

Page 69

1. **a)** **Who** – Grace Allbright; **What** – Arthur the cat turned up; **Where** – Her house, Miniver Avenue; **When** – Last night.
   b) 'Peaceful and still'.

Page 71

1. Informal.
2. To give a 'human angle' to the article.
3. 'she's got no car, there's no bus service and, in her own words she's 'a bit shaky on her pins'; 'the bus service, the village school, and the village bobby'.

Page 73

1. **a)** Parallel phrasing.
   b) Rhetorical question.
   c) Direct address/Second person.
   d) Rule of three.

Page 75

1. **a)** **Any from:** 'is devoted to', 'are dedicated to'
   b) **Any from:** 'would argue', 'must ask', 'could use', 'must value'.
   c) **Any from:** 'Newspapers, magazines and television', 'advice columns on how to attract the opposite sex, features on how to look your best and adverts for fashion and beauty products'.

Page 77

1. **a)** Present tense.
   b) A formal letter.
   c) 1. The classrooms 2. The corridors
      3. The foyer.
   d) She would like a reply and probably a meeting to discuss the issue.

Page 79

1. **a)** 'Warm comforting security blanket'
   b) 'And plunged… into what?'
   c) 'If all goes well, it could be the experience of your life'.

Page 81

1. **a)** 'Silence'.
   b) '…suggests something shaped…'.
   c) 'Perhaps… perhaps'/'something… something'.

Page 83

1. No. He says the reasons for it are 'a mystery'.
2. No. He feels the people he has spoken to are only 'following the party line'.
3. Past tense.

Page 85

1. **a)** He uses the pronoun 'we' and refers to the residents and their pressure group.
   b) However; Nevertheless.
   c) Also; Too; In addition.

Section A: Reading – Mark Scheme

Page 38: Foundation Tier Questions

Skills and Content

For each question, look at the mark schemes for achieving a grade D and a grade C, noticing how the **skills** that the examiner wants to see you using gradually build up. Note that you don't necessarily have to achieve every point in 'C' to get into that grade. Remember that if you are entered for Foundation Tier you will not be able to achieve a grade higher than C.

For each question, look at the suggestions of **content** that you might have included in your answer. You are not expected to have included all the suggested content, but you should have included most of it or other relevant points to achieve that grade.

Skills

1.

D	Three correct answers – see content suggestions on p.91.
C	Four correct answers – see content suggestions on p.91.

2.

D	• Show some evidence that you have understood the text. • Try to engage with the text. • Make some reference to information about the house and what happened to it mentioned in the text. • Give some relevant references or quotations to support your answer.
C	• Show clear evidence that you have understood the text. • Engage with the text and make inferences. • Make developed references to information about the house and what happened to it. • Give relevant quotations to support your answer.

3.

D	• Show some evidence that you have understood the text. • Try to engage with the text. • Make some reference to ideas about how to keep safe in the home. • Give some relevant references or quotations to support your answer.
C	• Show clear evidence that you have understood the text. • Engage with the text and make inferences. • Make developed references to information about how to keep safe in the home. • Give relevant quotations to support your answer.

4.

D	• Show some evidence that you have understood the language features of the text. • Make some comment on the effect of words and phrases used to argue. • Try to support your response with relevant quotations or examples. • Try to focus on language which argues.
C	• Show clear evidence that you have understood the language features of the text. • Clearly analyse the effect of words and phrases used to argue. • Give relevant quotations to support your answer. • Focus clearly on language which argues.

5.

D	• Show some evidence that you have understood the presentational features of the texts. • Try to compare the presentational features. • Make some comment on the effect of presentational features in both texts. • Try to support your points with appropriate examples.
C	• Show clear evidence that you have understood the presentational features of the texts. • Clearly compare the presentational features of the texts. • Clearly analyse the effect of the presentational features in both texts. • Support your points with relevant and appropriate examples.

Section A: Reading – Mark Scheme

Content

1. You may include:
   - It was a bungalow.
   - They bought it 30 years ago.
   - It fell down the cliff.
   - The cause was coastal erosion.
   - It was 500 yards from the edge when they bought it.
   - It had views over the North Sea.

2. You may include:
   - She felt helpless.
   - She looked to her husband for support.
   - She found it difficult to believe.
   - She accepts that there was nothing she could have done to stop it.
   - Her first reaction was shock and horror.

3. You may include:
   - The home can be a very dangerous place.
   - A lot of people end up in A&E because of accidents in the home.
   - Accidents can be easily avoided if you take care.
   - Slips, trips and falls can result in serious injury.
   - There are simple ways to help avoid accidents in the home.

4. You may include:
   - Uses first person ('I') to show it's a personal point of view.
   - Uses exclamation marks to show the strength of his feelings.
   - Uses rhetorical questions.
   - Gives examples from his own experience.
   - Uses exaggeration ('stolen her sweets').
   - Uses insulting language about people he does not agree with ('this harridan'; 'crazed head teacher').
   - Compares the dinner lady to a prison guard.
   - Uses 'we' to get readers on his side and invites them to give their response.

5. You may include:
   'My House Fell Off a Cliff!'
   - Bold clear headline.
   - Dramatic picture illustrating the article and emphasising the force of nature and emotive picture of Frances.
   - A strap line that explains the headline and a byline that shows it is a personal story.
   - Short, sharp subheadings in bold font and upper case letters that help to organise the story.
   - Short paragraphs.
   'Be Safe in Your Own Home!'
   - Colours, including red which makes us think of danger.
   - Dramatic images to emphasise the dangers.
   - Very short paragraphs for impact.
   - Clear, sharp subheadings in bold and upper case.
   - Bullet points and numbering used to organise the text.
   - Information box at the end.
   - Logo to show that it comes from a trusted source.
   'Now Health and Safety Really Have Gone Mad!!'
   - Clearly from a website.
   - No background colour or illustrations.
   - Links to other pages.
   - Arresting headline in bold.
   - Laid out in paragraphs but no subheadings – paragraphs comparatively long.
   - Hyperlink at end invites readers to respond.

Page 42: Higher Tier Questions

Skills and Content

For each question, look at the mark schemes for achieving a grade D to a grade A*, noticing how the **skills** that the examiner wants to see you using gradually build up. If you are doing everything in the A/A* you will be A*, while if you are achieving some of these points you are A. Similarly, all the B/C bullet points would give you B and just some of them a C.

For each question, look at the suggestions of **content** that you might have included in your answer. You are not expected to have included all the suggested content, but you should have included most of it or other relevant points to achieve that grade.

Skills

1.

D	• Show some evidence that you have understood the text.
	• Try to engage with the text.
	• Make some reference to the information given in the text.
	• Give some relevant references or quotations to support your answer.
B/C	• Show clear evidence that you have understood the text.
	• Engage with the text and make inferences.
	• Begin to interpret the text and make inferences.
	• Give relevant quotations to support your answer.
A/A*	• Show evidence that you fully understand the text.
	• Show a detailed engagement with the text.
	• Make perceptive comments and inferences from the text.
	• Give appropriate quotations or references to support your answer.

Section A: Reading – Mark Scheme

2.

D	• Show some evidence that you have understood the presentational features. • Try to link them with the text. • Give some explanation of why they are effective.
B/C	• Show clear evidence that you have understood the presentational features. • Make some clear and appropriate links between the presentational features and the text. • Use relevant quotations or references.
A/A*	• Give a detailed explanation and interpretation of the effect of the presentational features. • Link the presentational features to the text with perceptive comments. • Give appropriate quotations or references to support your answer.

3.

D	• Show some engagement with the text and the events described/the methods used to convince readers/the writer's argument. • Try to comment on and explain thoughts and feelings. • Give some quotations or references in support of your answer.
B/C	• Show a clear understanding of what is described in the text/the methods used to convince/the writer's argument. • Explain clearly and begin to interpret thoughts and feelings. • Use relevant quotations or references to support your answer.
A/A*	• Engage in detail with what is described in the text/the methods used to convince/the writer's argument. • Give perceptive explanations and interpretations of the thoughts and feelings expressed. • Use appropriate quotations or references to support your ideas.

4.

D	• Show some evidence that you have understood the texts' use of language. • Show some appreciation of the effects of words and phrases in different contexts. • Try to give appropriate quotations or references in support of your answer. • Try to compare the writers' use of language.
B/C	• Show a clear understanding of the texts' use of language. • Explain clearly the effect of words and phrases in different contexts. • Use relevant quotations or references to support your answer. • Make clear comparisons and cross references between the two texts.
A/A*	• Show full and detailed understanding of the texts' use of language. • Analyse how the writers have used language differently to achieve their effects. • Use appropriate quotations or references to support your ideas with perceptive comments. • Focus on comparison and cross referencing between the texts.

Content

1. You may include:
   • Daffodils have been known since about 300 BC.
   • They grew in the Mediterranean and the Middle East.
   • They were brought to Britain by the Romans.
   • For a long time they were seen as weeds.
   • They are perennials and grow from bulbs.
   • They grow best in climates with cold winters and cool springs.
   • They can grow 6–20 inches high.

2. You may include:
   • The picture of a nurse complements the text, which is written as if by her, using 'we'.
   • She helps to personalise the charity, making it about individual people.
   • She looks efficient and professional but friendly.
   • The daffodil emblem makes us think of spring and new hope, giving a positive message.
   • The yellow box picks up on the colour of the daffodil.
   • Blue, green and yellow are pleasant, soothing colours.
   • All the 'thank you's in the blue box look like handwriting, making it personal.
   • The nurse seems to be encouraging us to play the video.
   • The layout is clear and unfussy.

- Quotes from real people are included.
- Information about how donated money is used is highlighted clearly in a yellow box with clear icons.

3. You may include:
   - Early in the walk she and her companions felt like returning because the wind was so violent.
   - It was a difficult walk and they needed a lot of rests.
   - There was plenty to see on the walk, including plants which she found interesting and was able to identify.
   - She was impressed both by the quantity of daffodils and their beauty.
   - She felt that they were like happy people, dancing and laughing.
   - The daffodils gave the impression of 'simplicity, unity and life', providing a satisfying end to the walk.

4. You may include:
   'Daffodils'
   - It is essentially an information piece so there is a lot of 'factual' language, with dates and place names.
   - There is some 'specialised' language, which the readers (presumably gardeners) will understand, such as 'perennials'.
   - It begins with a rhetorical question to draw readers in.
   - It uses the first person plural pronoun 'we' and the second person pronoun 'you' at the start to involve the reader.
   - There is a quotation from Wordsworth but apart from that there is not much descriptive language.
   - The last part changes to the language of instruction, using imperatives to tell people what to do.
   - Finally there is a catchy slogan from the sponsors of the site.

'Marie Curie'
- It is written in the first person plural ('we'), making it personal and involving the reader.
- The headline ('Thank You') emphasises the charity's appreciation of donations and makes readers feel good before they are encouraged to donate.
- The text is very factual, without a lot of emotive language, making it seem professional and trustworthy.
- Statistics convey how much work the charity does as well as how much money it needs.
- It is very polite ('please' and 'thank you'), yet direct ('we need').
- It includes some imperatives.
- Quotes from people are included which highlight the charity's important work.

'Dorothy Wordsworth's Journal'
- It is written in past tense, as someone would write a diary at the end of the day.
- She does not always write in complete sentences, giving a sense of notes made straight after the event.
- There are a lot of short sentences, perhaps reflecting the 'stop/start' nature of the walk.
- She gives a list of flowers and plants, noting their variety and showing her knowledge of them.
- The daffodils are described in longer, flowing sentences, reflecting their impact on her.
- She personifies the daffodils, giving them feelings.

Section B: Writing – Mark Scheme

Page 86–87: Foundation and Higher Tier

Skills and Content

For each question, look at the mark schemes for achieving a grade D to a grade A*, noticing how the **skills** that the examiner wants to see you using gradually build up. If you are doing everything in the A/A* you will be A*, while if you are achieving some of these points you are A. Similarly, all the B/C bullet points would give you B and just some of them a C.

The mark scheme given here can be applied to all the questions on pages 86 and 87.

Remember that if you are entered for Foundation Tier you will not be able to achieve a grade higher than C.

D	You should:
	• Communicate ideas with some success.
	• Engage the reader with some detailed ideas.
	• Show awareness of the purpose and intention of writing.
	• Write in an appropriate tone (formal or informal).
	• Use devices such as rhetorical questions, lists and hyperbole if appropriate.
	• Use some words and phrases, including discourse markers, effectively.
	• Use paragraphs.
	• Use some structural features as appropriate, e.g. different paragraph lengths.
	• Show some control of agreement, punctuation and sentence construction.
	• Usually use accurate sentence demarcation.
	• Use a variety of sentence forms.
	• Accurately spell common words.
	• Use Standard English when appropriate.
B/C	You should:
	• Communicate ideas clearly and successfully.
	• Engage the reader with more detailed ideas.
	• Show clear awareness of the purpose and intention of writing.
	• Write in an appropriate tone (formal or informal) for the intended audience, beginning to use, for example, emphasis, assertion, reason and emotive language.
	• Use devices such as rhetorical questions, lists and hyperbole if appropriate.
	• Use words and phrases, including discourse markers, effectively.
	• Use paragraphs effectively.
	• Use a variety of structural features as appropriate, e.g. different paragraph lengths.
	• Show control of agreement, punctuation and sentence construction.
	• Use accurate sentence demarcation.
	• Use a variety of sentence forms.
	• Accurately spell most words.
	• Use a developed vocabulary.
	• Use Standard English when appropriate.

A/A*	You should:
	• Communicate ideas in a convincing and compelling way.
	• Engage the reader with a range of detailed and sophisticated ideas.
	• Show and sustain clear awareness of the purpose and intention of writing.
	• Write in an appropriate tone (formal or informal), which is increasingly subtle, for the intended audience using, for example, emphasis, assertion, reason, emotive language.
	• Use devices such as rhetorical questions and other rhetorical devices, hyperbole, irony and satire if appropriate.
	• Show control of an extensive vocabulary, including appropriately used discourse markers.
	• Use paragraphs effectively to enhance meaning.
	• Use a variety of structural features as appropriate, e.g. different paragraph lengths.
	• Use complex grammatical structures and punctuation successfully.
	• Use accurate sentence demarcation.
	• Use a variety of sentence forms.
	• Accurately spell ambitious words.
	• Use Standard English consistently when appropriate.

Accent – the way in which someone pronounces words, usually connected with a region.

Active voice – where the subject performs the action, e.g. 'The dog bites Tim'.

Adjective – a word which describes a noun.

Adverb – a word which describes a verb, often ending in 'ly'.

Advise – to recommend someone how to act (verb is *advise*; noun is *advice*; adjective is *advisory*).

Alliteration – repetition of a sound at the beginning of two or more words.

Analyse – to examine (noun is **analysis**).

Anecdote – a short personal story, given as an example.

Apostrophe (') – punctuation mark used to show possession or omission.

Article – a short piece of non-fiction writing in a newspaper or magazine.

Assonance – repetition of a vowel sound within words.

Attitude – someone's feelings or opinions.

Audience – a group of people who hear, read or see something, readership.

Authorised – official, allowed.

Autobiography – the story of the writer's own life.

Biography – the story of someone else's life.

Blog – a diary or journal published on the internet (short for 'weblog').

Blogger – a person who writes a blog.

Broadsheet – a 'serious' newspaper, traditionally in a large format.

Byline – the writer's name, usually on a newspaper or magazine article.

Chart – a sheet or block of information in the form of a table or diagram.

Chronological – the order in which things happen, following the time.

Clause – a group of words, including a main verb, that could stand as a sentence.

Colloquial – everyday, informal language.

Colon (:) – punctuation mark used to introduce a list or explanation.

Column – a vertical division of a page, most common in newspapers.

Comma (,) – punctuation mark used to divide items in a list or separate clauses or phrases in a sentence.

Complex sentence – a sentence consisting of more than one clause (but not a compound sentence).

Compound sentence – a sentence consisting of two clauses joined by a conjunction.

Conditional sentence – a sentence including 'if' and raising a possibility.

Conjunction – a word, such as 'and', 'but' or 'because', used to connect words or phrases in a sentence.

Connective – any word that is used to connect words or phrases.

Connotation – a meaning that is suggested by the use of a word or phrase.

Consonant – any letter apart from a, e, i, o, and u.

Content – subject matter; what something contains.

Contraction – the shortening of two words into one using an apostrophe, e.g. 'I'll' or 'doesn't'.

Counter argument – an argument given in response to another argument.

Critic – a person who reviews or criticises.

Cross-head – a word or phrase in bold, within the text, acting like a subheading in a newspaper or magazine.

Deduction – a conclusion, something worked out by the reader but not overtly stated by the writer.

Diagram – a sketch or drawing, usually labelled to help the reader understand how to do something or how something works.

Dialect – words or phrases particular to a region.

Diction – the choice of words and phrases used.

Direct address – speaking directly to the audience, usually using the second person, 'you'.

Direct speech – the actual words spoken, put in inverted commas.

Discourse marker (discursive marker) – word or phrase used to connect sentences or paragraphs and provide 'signposts' to guide the reader through the text.

Ellipsis (...) – punctuation (three dots) indicating that something has been omitted.

Embed – to include (quotations) as part of a sentence.

Emoticon – a small, simple drawing (e.g. a smiley face) used in texts and e-mails.

Emotive language – language used to provoke emotions in readers.

Encyclopedia – a book of information about many different subjects.

Evidence – information provided to support what the writer is saying.

Exclamation mark (!) – punctuation mark used to show extreme emotion.

Explain – to make something known or understood (noun is *explanation*; adjective is *explanatory*).

Fact – something that can be shown to be true or is accepted as being true.

Feature – an article in a newspaper or magazine that is not a news report.

Figurative language – language that describes something in terms of something else, e.g. using metaphor, simile or personification.

Font – the style and size of type used.

Footnote – an explanatory note or reference at the bottom of a page.

Form – the shape of something (e.g. leaflet), sometimes used as an alternative to 'genre'.

Formal – in accordance with rules or conventions.

Fragment – another word for a 'minor sentence', one which doesn't contain a main verb.

Full stop (.) – punctuation mark used to indicate the end of a sentence.

Functional writing – useful or everyday writing.

Genre – literally the 'kind' or 'type', used to categorise types of writing, e.g. romance, comedy.

Ghost writer – a writer who writes an 'autobiography' for another person but is not named as the author.

Graph – a diagram showing the relationship between two variables.

GUI widget – a link on a web page that enables readers to reply and give their views.

Guide book – a book that tells you about a place, intended for tourists.

Hard copy – writing printed on a page (e.g. a book rather than a website).

Headline – heading at the top of a newspaper/magazine article.

Homophone – a word that sounds like another word but is spelt differently and has a different meaning, e.g. bare/bear.

Hyperlink – a link in a web page that enables readers to connect directly to other pages.

Hyperbole – exaggeration.

Icon – a small picture to represent something.

Image – any visual representation, such as a picture, or an example of figurative language, such as a metaphor.

Imperative – a command, e.g. 'Get up!'.

Imperfect tense – the tense that describes an action in the past that is incomplete, e.g. 'I was running'.

Indent – to start writing in from the margin (noun is *indentation*).

Indirect speech – speech that is reported, not using inverted commas, e.g. 'She said that she would be late' (also known as reported speech).

Inference – a deduction from the text about something that is implied but not openly stated by the writer.

Informal – not formal, colloquial.

Inform – to provide facts (noun is *information*; adjective is *informative*).

Intention – purpose; what someone wants to do.

Interactive – something the reader can get involved with, particularly web pages.

Inverted commas (' ') – punctuation marks used to denote speech, quotations etc.; can be double or single.

Glossary of Key Words

Irony – humorous use of language, usually saying the opposite of what the writer really means (similar to sarcasm).

Jargon – vocabulary that is specific to certain fields/subjects, e.g. medical jargon (also called *technical language*).

Linguistic devices – language techniques; ways of using language.

List – a number of items or words put together.

Logo – the emblem of, for example a company, usually combining words and images.

Metaphor – a way of describing something by referring to it as something else, e.g. 'He's a little angel'.

Minor sentence – a 'sentence' which does not include a verb (also called *fragment*).

Modal verb – a verb such as 'might', 'may' or 'should' used with another verb.

Monochrome – in photography, black and white.

Narrative voice – the type of narrator, or storyteller, used.

Non-fiction text – any text that is factual not fictional.

Noun – a 'naming' word.

Object – the person/thing in the sentence that the verb is being acted on.

Omission – leaving something out, usually letters.

Onomatopoeia – the use of words that sound like their meaning, e.g. 'fizz' or 'crackle'.

Opinion – what someone thinks.

Paragraph – division of a text marked by the indentation of the first line or, in print, sometimes by leaving a line.

Parallel phrasing – repeating the structure and some of the words of phrases, clauses or sentences (also called *parallelism*).

Paraphrase – to put into your own words.

Parentheses – brackets; a word or phrase inserted into a sentence to explain something.

Passive voice – where the subject has the action done to him, e.g. 'He was bitten by the dog'.

Past perfect tense – tense used to convey the distant past, e.g. 'She had been an acrobat once' (also called *pluperfect tense*).

Past tense – any tense that describes something happening in the past, e.g. 'He walked' (simple past), 'He was walking' (past continuous), 'He has walked' (perfect) or 'He had walked' (past perfect).

PEE – a technique for organising a response to a text: make a point, give evidence, give an explanation. (Also called PEC (point, evidence, comment), PEA (point, evidence, analysis), 123, etc.)

Perfect tense – the tense that describes a completed action, e.g. 'He has walked'.

Personal pronoun – stand in place of names of people or things: I, we, you, he, she, it, they.

Personification – a kind of metaphor which gives human characteristics to a thing or idea, e.g. 'The tree wept for her', 'Death, be not proud'.

Persuade – to convince someone to do something or to feel a certain way.

Plural – more than one, e.g. 'they', 'we'.

Possession – ownership.

Post script (PS) – a note added to a letter after the signature, literally 'after writing'.

Preposition – words in sentences that show the relationship of one thing to another, e.g. under, towards, beside.

Present tense – any tense that describes something happening now, e.g. 'She walks' (simple present) or 'She is walking' (present continuous).

Preview – a short piece of writing looking ahead to an event that hasn't yet happened.

Pronoun – a word used as a substitute for a noun e.g. 'he', 'it', or 'them'.

Pun – a play on words, perhaps when two similar words have different meanings, usually used for humorous effect.

Purpose – intention or reason for doing something.

Question mark (?) – punctuation mark used instead of a full stop to show that a question is being asked.

Quotation – words or phrases taken directly from a text, shown by the use of inverted commas.

Recipient – a person who receives something, e.g. a letter.

Register – the form of language used in particular circumstances, e.g. formal or informal.

Relative pronoun – a word such as 'who', 'which' or 'that' used instead of a noun to connect clauses, e.g. 'I ate the cake, which didn't do me any good'.

Repetition – saying or writing something more than once.

Report – an account of something that has happened.

Reported speech – indirect speech.

Reverse chronological order – an order of events that starts with the present and goes backwards.

Review – a report by someone who gives an opinion about, for example, books or films.

Rhetoric – the art of speaking (adjective is *rhetorical*).

Rhetorical question – a question that doesn't expect an answer

Rhyme – the use of words which end with similar sounds, used at the end of lines of verse.

Rule of three – rhetorical device of using a list of three words or three phrases for effect.

Salutation – the greeting at the start of a letter.

Second person – 'you' (both in the plural and the singular).

Semi-colon (;) – punctuation mark used to connect clauses without using a connective; also used in lists.

Simile – figurative language used to describe something by comparing it to something else using 'like' or 'as'.

Simple past – tense which describes something that happened in the past, e.g. 'He walked'.

Simple sentence – a sentence that contains a subject and a main verb.

Slang – informal language, often local and often changing quickly.

Slogan – a catchy phrase often associated with a company or product.

Source – in the exam the text on which you base your answers.

Standard English – the variety of English accepted as the correct form for formal writing and speaking.

Statistics – numerical data.

Strap line – a subheading under the headline, which explains or expands on the headline.

Subheading – a word or phrase in bold or underlined, which breaks up and organises text.

Subject – the person or thing that a sentence is about.

Subjective – personal (in the context of an opinion or view).

Subordinate clause – a clause that adds extra information or explanation, but which isn't needed for the sentence to make sense.

Summary – a brief account which gives the main points (verb is *summarise*).

Superlative – an adjective describing the highest form of something, usually ending in 'est', e.g. slowest, brightest.

Tabloid – a type of newspaper, usually less 'serious' and easier to read than a broadsheet, traditionally in a smaller format.

Text box – a box containing text.

Text language – non-standard English used in texting or e-mails.

Third person – he/she/it (singular); they (plural).

Tone – the general feeling or mood of a text.

Topic sentence – a sentence, usually the first in the paragraph, which tells you what the paragraph is going to be about.

Unauthorised – done without permission (e.g. unauthorised autobiographies).

Verb – a 'doing, thinking, feeling or being' word.

Vocabulary – words.

Vowel – a, e, i, o or u.

Worldwide web – the communication network accessed through computers.